THE ART OF
SONGWRITING

THE ART OF SONGWRITING

How to Create, Think and Live Like a Songwriter

ED BELL

Bell, Ed
Book : The Art of Songwriting

Library of Congress Control Number: 2017906982

ISBN 978-0-9981302-0-0 (Paperback)
ISBN 978-0-9981302-1-7 (PDF eBook)
ISBN 978-0-9981302-2-4 (ePub eBook)

First published July 2017
New York City

WHY THERE ARE NO REVIEWS ON THIS PAGE

If you think I'm going to quote anyone's review here
you've missed the entire point of this book.

Seriously – read it yourself.

Form your own opinion.

I dare you.

CONTENTS

ABOUT THE SONG FOUNDRY

At The Song Foundry it's our mission to share great songwriting ideas with the world. At thesongfoundry.com we publish articles about songwriting, host free videos on various songwriting topics, and offer Skype songwriting coaching worldwide.

Connect with us online to find out more:

thesongfoundry.com

youtube.com/TheSongFoundry

facebook.com/TheSongFoundry

twitter.com/TheSongFoundry

INTRODUCTION:
WHAT THE $&%! IS THIS BOOK?

You've picked up this book. So you probably have some reasonable questions: What the $&%! is it? Who the &€#! wrote it? And why the $&#?%£! is it time for a new book on songwriting anyway?

Let's start in the middle, like *Star Wars*.

Hi. I'm Ed. I'm a musician and writer. I write a lot of music for theatre these days, but along the way I've written everything from straight-up pop music to rap music to avant-garde classical music where you had to climb inside the piano and hit the strings with a coin.

I'm also the kind of person who loves to figure out how stuff works. Ideally, I love to figure out that sort of stuff first-hand. And I love figuring that sort of stuff out because I love to use what I've learnt to create new stuff.

And one of the most important things I learnt from all of this figuring out is that creating different kinds of music isn't as different as you might think.

Sure, different types of music sound different. That's a no-brainer. You can write a song at the piano or you can write a song with a guitar or you can write a song on a laptop and never let it see a real-life instrument. They're all great ways to write a song and they'll all create something that sounds different. But while doing my fair share of creating different things, I started to realize that the big ideas you think about when you write a new song are more or less universal, whatever you happen to be working on.

It's kind of like building a house: whether you decide to paint the outside red or green or purple, you still have to think about the same sort of things to build a house that isn't going to fall down. And best of all, you don't necessarily have to learn all of that from building houses. You could learn it from building bridges or office blocks or replica medieval fortresses. Sure, whether you end up building in steel, brick or stone is going to affect what you think about. But underneath that you're going to be relying on some pretty much universal principles of construction to guide you.

And likewise, whatever kind of songs you're trying to create, whatever styles you want to work in – and whatever you learned already to get you here – lots of what you do as a songwriter comes down to a few key ideas.

Realizing that is kind of central to who I am, and looking at those key ideas is a big part of what the $&%! this book is.

We'll talk about the other parts later, but to get there we're going to have to look at why it's time for a new book on songwriting.

One of the other important things I learnt from doing lots of figuring out is that being good at figuring out is an important skill in itself. Sure, education is great. It's great to go to college or join a writing group or find a great mentor. Other people know things that you don't yet and it pays to find out what some of those things are. But as an artist, there are also things other people can't teach you. There are some things you can only figure out for yourself first-hand. And more often than not, it's this hard-won wisdom that makes all the difference in the end.

The thing is, as an artist you kind of have to be unique. There's no point being a carbon copy of something (or someone) that already exists. That means you have to carve out your own path, which also means nobody on this or any other planet can give you everything you're going to need to know. They don't – and can't – know it any better than you do.

So guess what? That means this one's on you.

That is, your job as an artist isn't to find yourself, whatever that means. It's to create yourself. You get to create yourself as the kind of artist and kind of person you want to be. You get to learn from and be influenced by people who know things you don't, but ultimately it's up to you to put all the pieces together in the way you decide to put them together. And, all things considered, that's your biggest and most important challenge.

It's also your toughest challenge. Not just because it's hard work. But because it's always a big leap into the unknown.

You might know this great line by Leonard Cohen: "Being a songwriter is like being a nun: you're married to a mystery."

And it's true: being a songwriter involves faith, dedication and absolutely no sex.

OK, one of those things isn't true. But there are lots of ways songwriting is just like religion. They're both puzzles you have to unpack in your own way. You get to practice both things by deciding what you believe and what it means to you and that's that. You get to decide whether you believe in God or Brahma or Cthulhu or ManBearPig or none or all of the above. There's no right or wrong. In a sense, what you believe doesn't matter anyway. What matters is that believing it makes your life better.

And that's key. If you've set your sights on a particular goal there are no right or wrong ways to get there. There are only things you can believe that are more helpful than others at getting you there. If you want to be an Olympic high jumper but you believe training is a waste of time and you'll just wing it on the day, it's probably not going to work out well for you. You've chosen a shitty belief that's not really compatible with your goal and as a result you're going to have a shitty time.

So although as a songwriter there isn't much that's definitively right or wrong, that doesn't mean it's a free-for-all. Like being a nun, there's a bit more to it than eat, sleep, pray and hope for the best.

On the one hand there are craft principles you have to learn: fundamental and mostly definitive ideas that are to do with how words and music work. Mastering these principles means picking up a ton of very literal skills you'll use to do your job properly.

And on the other hand there are more subjective beliefs you have to figure out: beliefs about who you want to be as an artist and the kind of art you want to make. These beliefs are definitely not definitive, but the way you start making your mind up about these things *is* pretty fundamental. There are things you can think about to help you get there, and that's what the hazier skill of creating yourself is all about.

But for some reason, it's a skill people don't talk about very much.

So I wanted to give it a try. I wanted to create a songwriting book that doesn't just talk about the craft of how songs are made, but also about the fuzzier, more mysterious – but just as important – parts of what it means to be an artist.

In fact, what most songwriting books won't tell you is that success as a songwriter – however you define it – is as much about how you live your life and the way you see the world as it is about your skill with words and music.

Maybe just let that sink in for a moment. It's a really important idea.

The key to creating like a songwriter is to think like a songwriter. Because action follows thought. But the key to thinking like a songwriter is to *be* a songwriter – to live your life like a songwriter, to see the world as a songwriter. Because thinking like a songwriter isn't just something you switch on when you sit down to write. It's part of who you are and how you think day in, day out.

In other words, you have to live creatively if you want to think creatively if you want to create creatively.

And in short, that's why it's time for a new book on songwriting. It's time to talk about songwriting from a new perspective. It's time to do justice to all of these important ideas that work together to make you a songwriter, not just the craft ideas that get talked about a lot. It's time to talk about the art – not just the craft – of songwriting.

So if this book is about big, universal ideas, that means it's supposed to be useful to you whatever kind of music you make. It's not a book about writing rock songs or gospel songs or rap songs. It's just a book about writing songs, and it's up to you to see how these ideas apply specifically to the music you want to make.

Because here's the thing: you probably have access to the best and most perfectly suited songwriting teachers you could ever want already – even if you've never met them. You're probably learning from them already. You're probably listening to their music. You're probably reading about them and watching them on TV and thinking about how they do what they do.

Everything you've ever wanted to know about songwriting is buried in the way these people live and think and create. The trick, of course, is knowing where to look – and, more importantly, what to look for.

And that's a pretty neat segue into what the $&%! this book is.

This book is a lens, a way of looking at songwriting, to make you the best self-teacher you could possibly be. It's here to make you better at thinking for yourself, solving your own problems and making things that no one's ever made before. It's here to challenge you to be the best version of the artist you are already.

This book is a way of talking about the fundamental principles of songwriting so that pretty much anyone – yes, anyone – can pick up the tools they'll need to go forth and make some really cool stuff.

And because this book is about the broader picture of what it means to be an artist, that's going to affect the way we look at these fundamental ideas. In at least three important ways.

Firstly, the focus of this book is more about asking you questions than giving you answers. If there are really no right answers – only your right answers – the worst thing I could do is try to give you some. Instead, we're going to talk a lot about how you come up with the answers yourself. We're going to talk about the kind of questions that can help you do that.

Secondly, it means it's not an academic book or a school book. It's not a book about analyzing songs and songwriting just for the hell of it. Sure, we are going to look back at what's been done, and we are going to take apart existing songs to see how they work, but we're going to look at those things only so that you can use them to make something new. It's one thing to explain how a jumbo jet flies. It's a totally different thing to explain how you design a new one.

Thirdly, I've tried to keep the ideas in this book simple. Partly because less is more, but also because these ideas *are* pretty simple. Like most things, songwriting's big ideas aren't that complicated, it's just using them that sometimes gets complicated. I'm going to use this book to tell you where to aim but then leave target practice up to you.

In fact, with creative things it's often better not to go into too much detail. Trying to juggle too many concepts at once can end up closing your mind more than opening it. You can get so comfortable overthinking that you end up doing more thinking than doing. So I'd much rather give you a few key concepts and let you take it from there. Sure, that means you'll make wrong turns and even big mistakes from time to time. But that's all good. Big mistakes usually contain the best lessons.

So there we go. That's what the $&%! this book is. We're almost at the point I can stop telling you about it and just let you enjoy it, but first let's get some basic housekeeping out of the way.

One: this book has fifteen chapters. They start with some general, big picture ideas, before focusing on more detailed, technical ideas, before zooming out for some big picture ideas again. It's your book so you get to do what you like with it, but the chapters often build on ideas I've talked about earlier, so I recommend you read them in order. Along the same lines, even if you write just music or just lyrics I recommend you don't skip anything. Whatever part of a song you contribute, it's still your job to understand how everything fits together, so you're not doing yourself any favors if you skip anything. (Plus, I saved some of the best jokes for these chapters. So there's that too.)

Two: it's not often I get super technical about how music is made, but when we do talk music I'm going to assume you have a basic knowledge of music theory. If not, that's OK, but it's worth finding a class or an online course or some other kind of magic learning device to help you pick up some of those skills – and not just for the sake of getting the most out of this book. (And yes, that applies to you too, lyrics-only writers.)

Three: I've been pretty selective about the detailed examples I put in the book, and whenever I've chosen them I've picked mostly older, well-known examples. I've done that because there's a good chance you'll know the songs I talk about already (and if not, you can easily get hold of them), though that doesn't mean you have to or ought to write exactly like them. But even more importantly, I've kept my examples pretty mainstream so that you can apply what I talk about to your own examples: to the music you love and want to learn from. That's an essential part of how this book works.

Four: unlike many similar books, there are no exercises at the ends of each chapter. That doesn't mean there are no conceivable exercises you could do after reading each chapter, it just means you should make your own up. You should take the ideas in this book and try them out in your own way or just try to use them in your next song. You'll have more fun and learn a lot more that way, I promise.

Five: there is some swearing in this book. You know that by now. If that offends you, I guess I could mention that people who swear are usually seen as more genuine and trustworthy. (Seriously, some scientists proved it.) I guess I could mention that if you want to be an artist you'll have to get used to being around people who swear, even if you don't yourself. But I'll just say sometimes you need those kinds of words to say what you need to say in the authentic and persuasive way you want to say it. *C'est la vie, mes amis.*

OK, that's our housekeeping over.

At this point it's traditional to say how fun writing this book was. And yes, it was a thrill. It was also frustrating, exhausting and occasionally mind-bending. It took way longer than I expected and there were plenty of times I had no idea if what I was writing was any good – as it is creating anything worthwhile.

But more importantly, writing this book was also really rewarding. It's not every day you get to make something that helps other people make something too. The best kind of thing to make.

So, *voilà*. Happy reading and – most of all – happy writing.

New York City

July 2017

THE ART OF SONGWRITING
IN BRIEF

As far as I'm concerned, all songwriting – all most things, actually – comes down to three simple, eternal principles:

Know your shit

Find out by trying

Be yourself

Know your shit means understanding how things work, what's already been done and how you might use it in future. It means doing your homework. It means ignorance is definitely not a virtue.

Find out by trying means knowing your shit won't give you all the answers. It means the only way to know something works is to keep trying different versions of it until it does.

Be yourself means understanding that knowing things and being good at using them is only half the picture. You have to be you too. You have to give us something that you and only you can give us. You have to give us something that's not just well-made, but different-made too.

Every idea in this book expands on one or more of these basic principles. I'll leave it to you to figure out which is which.

[1]

THERE ARE NO RULES

"Some people wish above all to conform to the rules, I wish only to render
what I can hear."
CLAUDE DEBUSSY

"If I'd followed all the rules, I'd never have gotten anywhere."
MARILYN MONROE

'Rules are for fools.'

'There are no rules, only tools.'

'Make a rule to break a rule.'

Let's take two lessons from the book of life, chapter one. One: people bloody love a rhymed one-liner. Two: in life and in art, there are no rules.

Most things in life – at least, the most interesting things in life – aren't governed by rules. Whatever people tell you.

That doesn't mean life is a mess, nobody knows anything and nothing ever makes sense. It just means that seeing the world in black and white won't do you any favors. It means that no rule exists without plenty of exceptions and caveats. But mostly it means that spending your life doing something because it's 'correct' and not doing some other thing because it's a 'mistake' isn't going to work out well for you in the long run. Especially if you want to be an artist.

Instead, as artists, it's much better to play with choices and results. That distinction is subtle but powerful, so let's talk about it.

If you're an artist, it's not so much that there's a rule that says 'Don't take a nap on the highway'. If you really want to, sure, go ahead. But anyone who's thought about it for even a second knows that if you do, the chances you won't live to tell the tale are pretty high. So you'll probably decide it isn't a good idea most of the time.

In the same way, there isn't really a rule that says 'Respect other people'. If you don't want to do it, be my guest. But anyone who's thought about it for even a second knows that if you're always mean to other people, the chances are pretty high that you'll have no friends, nobody to write songs with and nobody to pick you up when you're feeling down. So – assuming those things are important to you – it's probably your loss in the long run.

This is how life works. We make choices. And as long as you're prepared to accept the results, you get to make whatever choices you think best.

But where life gets really interesting is that you don't always know how a choice is going to turn out. Sometimes you're faced with lots of options – even lots of great ones – and it's not easy to decide which one to pick. Probably whatever you choose there will be some good consequences plus a couple of not-so-good ones too. It's rarely perfect or easy. You just have to use your best judgment, make your choice and accept what happens.

That's where experience comes in. All 'being experienced' means is that you've done something enough times you develop a really solid sense of how your choices might turn out. (We'll talk more about this in Chapter 2.) The more opportunities you get to make choices and see what the results are, the better you get at making similar choices in future.

Songwriting works just like this too. There are no rules. There is nothing that says 'You absolutely must do this, ideally while you also do that, and Jesus H. Christ you absolutely mustn't do that.' No. You get to call the shots. You get to make your own choices. You get to take a chance on all kinds of things you're not completely sure about, knowing you'll never be completely sure about them.

You'll never be completely sure about what you're making because whenever you create something new you're always heading into uncharted territory. No matter how much experience you have you're always figuring plenty of things out from scratch. You've never made this particular thing before so you can't know everything about it. You just have to keep at it while you figure things out by trial and error. (Mostly error, incidentally.)

Of course, there's an art to doing this well. In songwriting, like in life, you might never be able to predict any results with 100% accuracy, but you can still try. In fact, it's good to try.

You do that by picking up a set of tools to guide you. These tools are called principles. They're tried-and-tested ideas that say 'If you do this, this is probably the result'. You learn these principles because they're really valuable if you want to write clear and smart and interesting songs. You just have to remember they don't *make* you write clear and smart and interesting songs.

You understand the craft of the art form you want to work in because it helps make sure that what you create is well made. You wouldn't buy a table that isn't level because the legs are all different lengths. You'd insist the person who made it figured out some basic carpentry skills first. And that's the beauty of good craft: it makes sure what you're trying to make works on a fundamental level, so we can concentrate on what the thing is supposed to do or say in the first place.

But craft principles backfire when they become rules – when people want to see making art in black and white, or when people turn to craft to give them solid answers. Because craft principles are only supposed to give you questions – they're only supposed to guide you, that's all. Worst of all, rules backfire because they stop you experimenting. Principles remind you that experimenting is the only way forward.

The trouble is, rules are easier to understand. They're simple, comfortable and reassuring. 'Do this' is easy to follow because it doesn't leave any room for doubt. So people like to create and follow rules as a kind of shortcut to understanding things in a more subtle, nuanced way. People sell you books, courses and websites full of rules because they think turning everything into a few easy-to-follow steps is somehow doing you a favor.

But this comes at a price because all rules miss the point in one way or another. They describe the world as a perfect, predictable and totally understandable place. And anything that does that is a big fat lie. A dangerous, misleading, close-but-no-cigar lie. The world isn't always predictable and perfect: it's beautiful and messy and that's what makes it so interesting. Our most important task as artists is learning to deal with that, not following hard-and-fast rules because we're afraid of dealing with that.

But luckily, that task is pretty straightforward.

You learn and understand the so-called rules so you have them at your fingertips. They're the tools you'll need to make whatever you're trying to make. But once you understand the rules, it becomes your privilege – your duty – to decide when to use them, when to twist or distort them, and when to ignore them altogether. You get to take their advice but not be a slave to them. You get to decide when what you're making is best served by the so-called rules and when it definitely isn't.

In a nutshell: we make our own rules.

We use the so-called rules to draw our own conclusions. We make case-by-case decisions based on what we know about songwriting already. Sometimes we have to look at the ideas *behind* the so-called rules and draw our conclusions from there. But mostly we do this neat juggling act of understanding what's been done in our art form before we got here, while somehow using all of that to create something that's never existed before.

In a tinier, tidier nutshell: we learn to think for ourselves.

We make our own rules by thinking for ourselves.

It's not possible to be an artist unless you learn to think for yourself. It's not possible to be an artist unless you develop a healthy disregard for rules, tradition and authority. It's not possible to create something interesting, individual and remarkable unless you decide to care about something more important than playing by the rules.

And this is something you develop bit by bit, by the way. The more you question what you're told – the more you consider whether what you're told corresponds to the reality in front of you – the more independent you become. The more independent you become, the more confident being independent you become – and that's what really matters.

> "A lot of people never use their initiative because no one told them to."
> BANKSY

So, in case you were wondering, this isn't going to be a book of rules. If you were looking for a book of rules – if you wanted a book that makes everything formulaic and really easy for you – you're going to be really disappointed. (With life, as well as this book.)

Instead, this is going to be a book of principles, ideas and tools.

There are no hard-and-fast rules in this book just like there are no hard-and-fast rules in life. And as with all principles, ideas and tools, it's your job to use the ones that are useful to you and mercilessly discard the rest.

It's that simple.

And here's a personal tip: if thinking for yourself means you discard half of what I've written, I won't even mind.

In fact, I'll be proud of you.

FUNDAMENTAL SONGWRITING CHALLENGE #1

Get to know the principles that tend to make great songs.

Then do whatever the $&%! you like with them.

[2]

THE LEARNING CURVE

"If people knew how hard I had to work to gain my mastery, it would not seem so wonderful at all."

MICHELANGELO

OK, real talk: learning something new is hard. Getting good takes time. And meanwhile – you're going to mess up. A lot.

More often than not, when you start learning something new you do it because you looked at someone who's great at it and you decided to give it a go too.

But once you start, it turns out to be much harder than you expected. Sometimes you can't help but take a look at how you're doing and ask yourself 'How the $&%! do they do it?'. You can't help wondering if what those people are doing is magic.

But it's not magic. Like all magic, it only looks like magic when you don't know how it's done. The people you want to emulate aren't somehow superhuman and gifted with special, superhuman powers. They're no more superhuman than you. They're probably just better at it for one simple reason: they've had a lot more practice.

Maybe that sounds obvious. But since it's the most important thing nobody tells you when you're starting out, here it is again: anyone who's really good at something has had a lot of practice at it. That's just how it works.

And here's the best part: one day the people you admire were no better at what they do than you are right now. They had to have been. Nobody jumps out of the womb, paintbrush in hand, ready to rattle off the *Mona Lisa* before they're even two hours old. Everyone has to start from scratch. No exceptions.

So whatever your dream is – to paint the next Mona Lisa, to build the next Empire State Building, just to get to Level 2965 on Candy Crush Saga – you're going to have to get there step by step. By making pencil drawings of fruit bowls, or by going to architecture school, or just by getting through Level 1 first.

And whatever happens, if you want to reach Level 2965 – in anything – you're going to have to stick at it. You've got to build the foundation, bit by bit, that's going to let you get to those higher levels. It was as true for the people you admire as it is for you. There aren't any shortcuts if you want to do it properly.

The trouble is, we live in a world where people throw around words like 'genius' and 'prodigy' like they're going out of style. Where lots of people think you're either born 'talented' or you're, well, not. Where lots of people think some of us are born at Level 1, but some of us strike it lucky and are born at Level 952, 1821 or 2547.

But it doesn't work like that. Ask your local 'genius' and they'll tell you. They'll tell you how hard they had to work to get good at what they do. They'll remind you how long it took them to get there. They'll tell you they weren't always this good at what they do.

Because when it comes down to it, the harder you work – and the more experienced you become – the more talented you seem to become. Just like the harder you work – and the more experienced you become – the more luck you seem to have too.

And sure, in the real world, chance plays a big part too. Some people have access to great opportunities or great mentors that help them make much quicker progress climbing up the levels than they would otherwise. But none of that affects the thing that's most important: the more you stick at something, the better you get at it.

Anyone can learn to be more creative. Anyone can learn to understand the craft of songwriting better. Anyone can start putting together all the different things you have to think about to be a great artist, and anyone can start creating things they had no idea they were capable of making.

What sucks is that lots of people don't know this yet. They're stuck believing they're as good an artist as they'll ever be and that's that. They try to do something creative and when things don't turn out as well as they hoped right away, they assume that means they'll never be any good. They assume they're just not cut out to be an artist. So they do what any self-respecting person who believes those things would: they give up.

But of course they're not very good yet. Nobody is very good when they're just starting out.

And that's the biggest problem with seeing the world that way. That's the reason plenty of people who like the idea of being an artist don't become artists. And I don't blame them. They just don't know any better. They just don't know that if you want to be a great artist, you have to put up with being a pretty terrible one first.

That's right: the only way to become great at something is to be happy being bad at it first.

The thing is, we learn by doing. We don't really learn by thinking, theorizing or staring out the window daydreaming about doing. All of these things play a part, but it's getting stuck in in the arena – in our case, writing and writing and writing – where you really learn what's what.

Here's how it works:

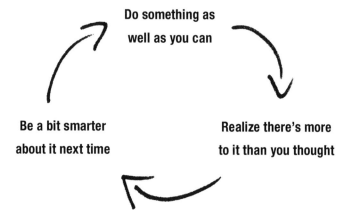

Do something as well as you can

Realize there's more to it than you thought

Be a bit smarter about it next time

You do things. You learn more. You get smarter. The cycle goes round and round. And the more it goes round, the better you get.

In Chapter 1 we talked about how life and songwriting are about choices and results. And we talked about how experience helps you make better choices and get better results. This cycle is that idea in action.

At the heart of this idea is that gap – the moment you do something and suddenly see a bit further than you could before. It's your reward for trying out something new. It's your reward for going out of your comfort zone.

And the way to climb the learning curve – the only way – is to stack as many of these little gaps on top of each other as you can. That's why real learning is done by doing. Every time you write something new you get a bit smarter about writing. And a bit smarter the next time. And even smarter the time after that.

> "In theory there is no difference between theory and practice.
> In practice there is."
> YOGI BERRA

Some people say it's a bad idea to compare your journey as an artist – or as anything – with anyone else's. It's your journey and nobody else's matters, right?

But what really makes comparing your journey to someone else's a bad idea is that it's almost never a fair comparison. You're different people. You've had different experiences and different opportunities. Chances are, if you'd got the same amount of experience and you'd landed the same opportunities as the person you're comparing yourself to, you'd be doing similar things.

So if you're not happy with what you're creating right now, if you wish you could do it differently, or if you wish you could do it better, that's totally OK. In fact, it's totally normal. Just keep writing. Let yourself off the hook and keep writing. Or don't let yourself off the hook and keep writing. Either way, just keep writing.

And don't ever assume that all the great artists you admire haven't been there too. Don't ever assume they never made something they didn't like. And definitely don't assume that they didn't write plenty of songs that sucked when they were starting out. Of course they did. You just don't get to hear them because they never made them public.

Just like your average social media account, what people share in public is a tiny fraction of all the other stuff going on behind the scenes. Just because you can't see the half-baked, average-but-promising songs your heroes wrote when they were still getting to grips with their art form, it doesn't mean those songs don't exist.

So wherever you are in your quest to reach Level 2965 – or whatever level you've got your eyes on – your only job is to focus on getting better. Not on being good. On getting better. However you can, and as much as you can.

And, once again, it's action that makes that progress happen. That's really important. No course, no mentor, no book – including this one – can make you a better writer on its own. Only you can make yourself a better writer – by writing.

So it's up to you to take the ideas in this book and, to paraphrase Monty Python, get the $&%! on with it. To do something – anything – with them. To use them on projects that inspire and excite you. To use them until you understand these ideas inside out. To use them so much and so well they're there at your fingertips whenever you need them.

Sure, this is a slow process. A really slow process. A process so slow that even calling it a slooooooooooooooooowwww prooooooooooooceeeeesss doesn't do justice to the years and years – usually at least a decade – it takes to become a great artist.

And it's a process that you never really finish, either. You're always picking up new ideas. You're always rediscovering old ones. You spend your whole life as an artist learning and changing and ripening into something new. That's one of the things that makes being an artist so exciting.

But the best thing about this kind of steady progress is it's the kind of progress that lasts. Once you've put in the hard work, the skills you end up with never really go away. In other words, once you've got those skills, you get to spend the rest of your life using them to make some really exciting stuff. Pretty cool, huh?

And let's not forget, songwriting is tough. It's not like doing accountancy or plastering or acupuncture. You don't just pick up three or four core skills you use day in, day out. You never quite settle into a daily grind. You have dozens of different skills to master and every time you try create something new you end up using those skills in completely different ways.

Nobody gets good at that overnight. You have to keep practicing every single skill, over and over. Even if you think you suck. *Especially* if you think you suck.

You've got to press on anyway. It's the only way to get there.

FUNDAMENTAL SONGWRITING CHALLENGE #2

Put in the work to master your art form.
It'll take a while, but it'll be worth it.

[3]

BEING AN ARTIST

"Artists use lies to tell the truth. Yes, I created a lie. But because you believed
it, you found something true about yourself."

ALAN MOORE, *V for Vendetta*

Here's something that's good to know: songs aren't just words that sort of rhyme
and sort of scan. Songs aren't just pretty sounds that distract us from everything
that's going on in the real world. The best of them are *about* the real world. They tell
us something about real life.

Part of being a songwriter is being an artist. And part of being an artist is
channeling your life experiences into what you make. Part of your job as an artist is
to turn life into art.

Lots of songwriters do this directly. They write about things that happened to
them first-hand. They write songs about how they're feeling and what they want and
what they think about what's going on in the world.

Other songwriters do it less directly. They write songs about other people or for
other people to perform. But in the process, they can't help but filter all of this
through their own ideas and experiences. If they try to write a love song, their

experiences of being in love will inform and affect what they write. All they've heard, read or seen about other people being in love will probably work its way in there too. And that's exactly how it's supposed to work.

In other words, whatever you write and whoever you write it for, it's your job to inject the real world into what you create.

If you write a love song, your challenge is to turn what love feels like into art. If you write a breakup song, your challenge is to capture what breaking up feels like. If you write a party song, your challenge is to create a song that feels like a party.

This doesn't have to be complicated. A love song that's a dance track probably won't explore being in love as deeply as a big power ballad might. And that's OK. As always, different genres apply these ideas in different ways.

But creating art that has some kind of relationship with real life is a big part of your job as a songwriter. It's what gives what you write meaning. It's what makes what you write real. And it's one of the things that makes what you write really worth paying attention to.

Think about the songs that have affected you in profound or important ways. Think about the songs that taught you things about life. Think about the songs that challenged you to think in a different way. And think about the songs that picked you up when you were down or feeling lonely, or the album that got you through that rough breakup.

That's what art can do. That's how art changes lives. And it's your job – not just as a songwriter, but as an artist – to find a way to do that in what you create.

In other words, the raw material of songwriting isn't music and words. It's life. And the better you understand life, the more powerful songs you'll create.

Writing is a test of your humanity, your understanding of what the world is, and maybe even your vision of what it could be. These things have a way of working their way into what you write – often in really subtle ways. And they're usually the difference between art that's just OK and art that's really powerful and meaningful.

That means part of becoming a better artist is becoming a better human being too.

That is, if you want to write about meaningful and interesting things, you have to try to understand them first. And if you want to try to understand them, you have to pick up the life experience (and life experiences) that are going to help you do that.

The best way to do that is to keep opening yourself up to as many new experiences as you can. Do things you've never done before. Take bigger risks than you've ever taken before. Get to know the kinds of people you'd never normally hang out with. See what people who aren't like you can teach you. Work harder than you ever have to understand the world from other people's points of view. Best of all, start doing all of these things and start calling it research.

You'll find out more about what it means to be human. You'll begin to figure out that all people – no matter who they are, where they are, or how they live their day-to-day lives – have a lot in common. (If that sounds like a nice idea in theory but you have no idea what it means in practice, just sit tight. We'll come back to it in Chapter 4.)

All of this, of course, is just another way of expressing a really fundamental idea: that all artists are observers. In one way or another, all artists *have* to be observers. Your job as an artist is to observe as much of the real world around you as you can, let it be filtered through your personality, your tastes, your ideas about what art should or shouldn't be, and use that as the raw material for all the art you're going to create.

And that, in short, is your challenge. Open your eyes. Open your heart. Figure out what you can see and write about it. Figure out what you think and believe about life, love and everything, and find ways to share those ideas in your songs.

"Make visible what, without you, might perhaps never have been seen."
ROBERT BRESSON

Your job as an artist is to let these things wind up in the art you make. They're the things that make up what people call your truth.

Not the truth – your truth.

I'll explain.

There are hard-and-fast truths in the world. These are things like how many arms I have, how far it is from here to Calcutta and how many coffees I had to drink to get through writing this chapter. They're objective truths that are hard to argue with. But there are also more subjective truths – like what you think love is, what you think a life well spent is, what you think is worth writing about. They're truths that say something about the way you see the world. They're truths that say something deeper about who you are as a person.

And these are the kind of truths we want to hear about in the things you make. (They're often also the kinds of things that motivate you to get writing in the first place.)

In fact, the more you inject your truth into what you make, the more a really remarkable thing happens: people start to find their own truth in what you've made. They start to be challenged or reassured or enlightened by what you've made. Some of them start to become subtly different people because of what you've made – maybe in the way you expected or maybe in a different way altogether.

And sure, not everyone will go crazy over what you make – we'll talk more about that when we get to Chapter 14. But you have to start sharing your truth in the most authentic and genuine way you can if you want to find out who your art is going to affect.

In short, artists are people who take on this monumental task of sharing their truth with everyone else. They're the kind of people who are not only smart enough to make observations about real life, but also daring enough to start turning those observations into art.

In other words, artists learn to be really good at tapping into the most interesting and exciting parts of being human. That's what making art – and being an artist – is all about.

FUNDAMENTAL SONGWRITING CHALLENGE #3

Write songs that capture real life and express something about what it's like to be human.

[4]

SONG DESIGN

"Plans are nothing. Planning is everything."
DWIGHT D. EISENHOWER

A big part of being an artist is having something to say. That's what the last chapter was about. But the other big part is finding ways to say it. That's our focus for the next few chapters.

We'll get into some details about how this works soon enough, but first we've got some bigger picture ideas to talk about. First up, the essential skill of deciding what your song is going to be about – the art of what I call song design.

Just like a painter makes sketches or an author plans out their novel, as a songwriter making a song is much easier once you've made a few key decisions about what your song is going to be. So let's get some key principles straight.

UNITY

The art of making pretty much anything is putting together lots of individual parts so that they work as a single integrated whole. You want to feel like every part of a work of art inevitably belongs together. You want to feel like every part is working together towards some larger goal.

This is the principle of unity. And in songwriting, that comes down to one big idea above all: a song is most effective when it's about one thing. And, well, whatever one thing you decide your song is about is usually the common thread that ties all of the song's different parts together into a single whole.

In practice, this is usually your song's thesis – its main idea or message. It could be something like 'I love you' or 'I miss you' or 'I'm a Barbie girl, in a Barbie world'. And, just like in these examples, the acid test of whether you've found a good central idea for your song is whether you can summarize what the entire song is about in a single sentence.

This thesis is the larger goal you want your song to pull off. And you'll often find that not only does the song's music have something to do with this main idea – we'll talk about that in Chapter 8 – but that every line of a song's lyric somehow relates to this big idea too.

That's an important concept, so let's see how it works. Here are the first four verses of a song you probably already know, 'Amazing Grace':

Amazing Grace, how sweet the sound,
That saved a wretch like me.
I once was lost but now am found,
Was blind, but now I see.

'Twas Grace that taught my heart to fear,
And Grace, my fears relieved.
How precious did that Grace appear
The hour I first believed.

Through many dangers, toils and snares
I have already come;

'Tis Grace that brought me safe thus far
And Grace will lead me home.

The Lord has promised good to me,
His word my hope secures.
He will my shield and portion be,
As long as life endures.

Sure, eighteenth-century hymns might not be the sort of songs you're bursting to write, but let's look at what these sixteen lines are saying.

Yes, the word 'grace' is in there a lot. But even when it's not there – like in the fourth verse – the song is still talking about the same thing: some guy being redeemed by his faith in God. You might summarize the whole song with the sentence 'The Lord's Grace saved me'. And you can tell that's a good summary because every line – and every word – plays a part in expanding on that simple unifying idea. The song basically expresses the same central thesis over and over in different ways.

And while it's one thing to sit here and admire how much someone else's song stays on topic, pulling this off in practice isn't always as easy as it looks. That's why having a strong sense of what your song is about is important: it helps you know what you're supposed to be writing about. It helps you decide what ideas to include in a song. And it helps you know when what you write is veering off track.

Of course, that doesn't mean you absolutely have to have figured out what your song is about before you write a single note or word. Sometimes you'll have enough of an idea to start writing and then refine or focus your central idea as you go. But what's important is that your song finds its focus in the end. It's not usually a good idea to try cramming two or three or twenty big ideas into one song – no matter how good those ideas all are.

So you could write a great song that says 'I love you because you're beautiful' or 'I love you because you're fun' or even 'I love you because you're Swedish', but part of deciding what your song is about is settling on just one of those things. Yep. Just one. Sure, you could write a song that says 'There are so many reasons I love you', but then that's still a single unifying idea – even if it's a broader one – to work with.

It might feel tough to throw away some of your best ideas to focus on just one of them, but your song will be all the better for it, I promise.

And as you know by now, don't just use my examples to help you understand this in practice. Start applying this principle to the songs you know and want to emulate. Try to summarize what each song is about and see how tightly the rest of the song relates to that central idea. Try to figure out how that single starting point might have inspired or generated the material in the whole song. You might be surprised by what you discover.

SONGS TELL STORIES

Here's some good news: your next song can be about virtually anything. There's nothing to stop you writing a song based on a central thesis like 'Toast is brown' or 'Cardiff is a nice place' or 'The cat flap was invented in 1721'.

But if you wrack your brain for a moment, you probably can't think of many songs that talk about those kinds of things. And there's a good reason for that: songs aren't usually just about anything. No. Songs tell stories.

That doesn't mean you should start your next song with 'Once upon a time'. It doesn't mean your next song should be a gargantuan epic about some guy's quest to save the world from fire-breathing monsters, corporate greed and people who think it's cool to create social media accounts for their pets.

It just means that songs are about people. Songs are about things that people say to each other. Songs are about people who have some kind of relationship – maybe they're dating, maybe they're friends, maybe one of them is an artist telling something to their fans. And songs are usually based on something that happened – or something that's happening – to those people.

These are the building blocks of great stories, and while different songs use these ideas in different ways, understanding that songwriting is a form of storytelling is a really powerful way of writing great material.

Think about a song like 'I Will Always Love You'. It's not just somebody saying 'I will always love you'. It's a song about a woman who loves a guy who doesn't love her back. That's a story.

Or think about a song like 'Born in the USA'. Sure, from the title you might think it's just a song about being proud to be American. But there's a bit more to it than that. It tells the story of a guy drafted to fight in Vietnam and how he feels about that. (Spoiler alert: not good.)

OK, I picked two songs that tell pretty substantial stories to explain my point, but you can work with much simpler stories too. Faithless's 'Insomnia' basically tells the story 'I can't get no sleep' and there's not much more to it than that. Sometimes the story is daft – like 'We all live in a yellow submarine' – and sometimes the story isn't really clear or is just bizarre – like whatever you decide 'I Am the Walrus' is about – but in virtually any song you can name you'll find some kind of story there. Again, there's some kind of situation that involves one or more people, and the song is about something that happened or is happening to those people.

The thing is, people love a good story. We love to know about the other stuff people are thinking about and all the stuff they're going through. And we're affected and captivated by stories more than anything else. If you look at the most stirring political speeches, the most inspiring TED Talks, and even the most persuasive TV ads, you'll almost certainly find the people who created them using stories to get their point across.

And songwriting is no different. More often than not, the best and most powerful songs don't just sound great: they're based on really great stories.

And when it comes to figuring out the story your next song is about, here are four fundamental and related questions that can help you do that:

- Who is singing?
- Who are they singing to?
- What are they trying to say?
- Why do they want to say it?

The first two questions come as a pair and they're usually the most straightforward to answer. I already mentioned how a song is sung from someone to someone else. You've gotta figure out who is who. Maybe it's a love song from one person to another. Maybe it's an artist telling us a story about someone interesting. Maybe it's an artist setting the record straight with the world, or at least anyone who'll listen.

The third and fourth questions also come as a pair, but your answers can be anywhere from really simple to much deeper and more nuanced. In short, the questions are about not just what the person singing your song wants to say – the song's thesis – but also where they might be coming from in saying it, what might be driving them to say it. You can probably think of a handful of reasons someone might feel driven to sing a love song. Or if a song is a story about someone else, maybe it's sung because it's a good story, or an uplifting story, or a sad story that's a warning to the rest of us. Or if it's just an artist setting the record straight with the world, it's probably because there's something worth setting straight.

As always, there are no right or wrong answers to these questions. All that matters is that the answers you come up with work well together as a whole. This is where all of the real life stuff of Chapter 3 comes in: your challenge is to find four answers that make sense together and ring true to real life.

Like, if you had to rewrite 'I Will Always Love You' as a song from a woman to a man she'd only met for five minutes, changing your answer to the second question means you also have to change what she's trying to say and why she wants to say it, because she probably wouldn't say something so strongly and so passionately to someone she didn't know well. Or if she was singing to someone who didn't have to leave, that would affect what she's trying to say as well as why she wants to say it – the thing that's driving her to say it.

That's what I mean when I say these four questions are related: more often than not, changing your answer to one of them means changing your answer to at least one of the others.

And to say it again – that the answers you come up with to these questions can be really simple. Someone saying something as straightforward as 'I love you' to their significant other because they're in love is absolutely a solid answer.

Oh, one more quick thing. There's a common songwriting idea that says part of song design is picking a single tense (past, present or future), viewpoint (first, second or third person) and voice (whether the person singing is singing to someone or just thinking out loud) for your song. And if thinking about this sort of thing helps you write, go for it. Absolutely. But you'll often find that answering the four questions I gave you gives you answers to these kinds of questions automatically.

In fact, you'll find plenty of songs that make great use of different tenses, voices or viewpoints throughout. There's no hard-and-fast rule that says no changing is allowed. There's only the general principle that having a single story or situation to sing about is a great way of unifying everything that goes into your song.

So there you go. There's your guide to how songs tell stories.

As always, these ideas are pretty much universal, but the way you apply them depends on the kind of music you want to create. Different genres tend to tell different kinds of stories, in different ways. So as always, the best way to understand this in practice is to apply these big ideas to the songs you admire and see what you can learn from that. What stories do those songs tell? What situations do those songs conjure up? And how might those songs answer the four fundamental questions we talked about?

The more you think about how this works in other people's songs, and the more you practice it in your own, the more exciting song ideas you'll find yourself coming up with.

WHAT MAKES A GOOD SONG IDEA?

So if songs tell stories, does that mean you can pick any old story to write about? Sure. Of course you can.

But it's no secret that some types of material makes more compelling subject matter than others. Some stories are more interesting to hear about than others. As always, there are no definitive rules, but since finding interesting subject matter is a big part of your song's success, here are a few important principles worth thinking about.

WRITE ABOUT WHAT INTERESTS YOU

Most of all, go with material that interests you. Challenge yourself with new things, but find challenges that interest you. It's impossible to tell for certain what will interest other people, but if it interests you, that's a good sign. If it makes you smile, if it makes you think or if it makes you cry, that's a good sign. If it's the sort of thing you'd be excited to tell your mates about, that's a good sign too.

Of course, the other advantage of writing about things that you're passionate about is that you'll do a much better job of it. A passionate writer with average material will almost always do a better job than an unenthusiastic writer with great material. That's worth bearing in mind.

WRITE ABOUT THINGS THAT AREN'T OBVIOUS AND EVERYDAY

Otherwise, it's worth searching for subject matter that's distinctive, unusual or different somehow. Small talk doesn't usually make interesting song material. The superficial, lame, everyday stuff that bored people talk about because they have nothing better to do doesn't usually make interesting song material.

Soon enough we'll talk about writing about things that resonate with lots of people, but that doesn't mean you have to pick the boring and everyday stuff people can associate with.

Go where the unusual or important stories are. Find unusual and interesting situations. Find stories with strong emotions. Find stories with mixed or layered emotions. Find stories about people who are different or people who see the world in interesting and individual ways. Or find stories that seem everyday in lots of respects, but approach them in a unique or different enough way that keeps them fresh and exciting.

Just like it's a journalist's job to find an interesting scoop or angle for a story, it's your job to ask yourself what it is that's fun or interesting or moving about the song you want to write. What does your song have to reveal that we don't hear about much? What story is worth dedicating three or four minutes of a song to?

DON'T WORRY ABOUT TELLING THE LITERAL TRUTH

That said, unlike a journalist, it's not necessarily your job to tell stories that are completely and utterly true. We touched on that idea in Chapter 3.

Lots of songs are based on the literal truth – they're about things that literally happened or are literally happening. But lots of songs aren't – they're either adapted from the truth or completely made up. And that's OK. All that matters is that they *could* be true – that we believe they could have happened.

So if you fell in love with a brown-eyed girl once, you could write a song about that. But the song could just as easily be about a blue-eyed girl or a brown-eyed boy and we'd still believe it. Or it could be about a brown-eyed girl who ran off with someone else after a month and broke your heart, even though that never literally happened. It doesn't matter, as long as it's a thing that could be true. It doesn't matter, as long as it's not a song about someone with seventeen eyes, or about someone you were completely in love with who left but it didn't bother you at all, because then we might not believe what you're talking about.

But most of all: don't just assume that writing about something that's literally true is an automatic ticket to a great song. I ran out of shampoo this morning, but I wouldn't write about it. Yes, as a songwriter you're an observer, and it's your job to turn real life into art. But it's also your job to sift through real life to find the things that are really worth turning into songs.

LOOK FOR SPECIFIC SITUATIONS WITH UNIVERSAL RESONANCE

In fact, that brings us to an important principle about choosing great subject matter: great songs tend to be about specific situations with universal resonance.

The trick to choosing great song material is pulling of a particular juggling act: writing about something that's both specific and universal at the same time.

The specific situation – whether it's literally true, completely invented or somewhere in between – is important because it makes the world of a song definite and real. 'Being in love' is a nice philosophical idea, but it's much better as a song idea when it's a specific person saying 'I'm in love'.

In fact, it's even better when we know a few more details about that specific person or about the specific situation they're in. Those details are what make a song unique and distinct from every other song ever written. No great love song is just any old love song. You couldn't just swap them with any of the fafillion other love songs that exist and not notice the difference. They're different because they're about specific people in specific situations with specific things to say. They're distinctive because whoever wrote them set themselves the specific challenge to write one particular song about one particular situation.

But at the same time, it's a song's deeper resonance that draws us into it in the first place. A song's specific situation might be someone else's business, but we're really good at seeing our business in there too. That's why we love to hear stories about other people. We want to see what they have in common with us.

That's why all that stuff about writing genuinely and authentically from your own experiences in Chapter 3 is so important. When you genuinely and authentically turn your own experiences into art, other people will see their own experiences in what you write. They'll be drawn to it because it resonates with them. They'll be drawn to it because deep down they'll see the truth – the kind of truth we talked about in Chapter 3 – in what you write.

'I Will Survive' is a great song idea because lots of people can associate with bouncing back after a devastating breakup. 'Dance With My Father' is a great song idea because lots of people can associate with wishing someone who died was still here – whether that person is a parent or someone else they were close to. And even if you've never literally found yourself pregnant and having to ask your parents for help, 'Papa Don't Preach' is a great song idea because lots of people can associate with being in a tough spot and being nervous about telling their family about it.

Sure, it helps that songs like these are written in a genuine and authentic enough way that it's easy for us to get inside their situations. But it also helps that these songs are about common enough things in life that you already understand their deeper themes and ideas. They're like making a new friend you feel like you've known your whole life. They make you go 'Yes, life is like that. That's definitely a thing that happens.' And that matters. It's part of what makes a great song idea really compelling.

And what's more, that means universal resonance isn't something you create. It's something that exists already, and it's your job to tap into it. It's your job to understand what kinds of things lots of people can associate with – on a deeper level – and prioritize writing songs about them.

So that's the neat trick of great song design. You want the specifics to make your song unique and to help you make the specific choices that will make the music and lyrics of your song extra distinctive. But you also want the universal resonance so that your specifics have meaning to lots of people.

And don't forget, if you're not sure where to find great song ideas, just look around. They're happening to you, they're happening to the people you know, they're happening to people who are in the papers and on your TV screens and on whatever else has been invented by the time you're reading this. And like we talked about, you can tweak and adapt these literally true stories as much as you like. You can use them as inspiration to tell the stories that interest you. You can even reinvent real-life stories completely. They're all great ways of turning the raw material of real life into your next song.

You've just got to keep your eyes open to the world to have somewhere to start from. And once that becomes second nature, you'll never be short of great things to write about.

FUNDAMENTAL SONGWRITING CHALLENGE #4

A big part of your song's success is having great subject matter.
Find some great material to write about.

[5]

THE CREATIVE PROCESS

Here's something fun to know about how creativity works: we don't really know how creativity works.

How exciting is that? How inspiring is that? Your brain can come up with things that have never existed before and nobody can completely explain how it does it. Somehow, it just does. Somehow, it can take in everything it's ever learnt or experienced and turn all of that into something new.

Creating something original is always going to take you somewhere unexpected. By definition. So that also means that the process that's going to take you there is going to be unpredictable, and that's totally the point.

But if you can't always plan where your creative brain will take you, you can learn to tweak and streamline your process to help your brain work at its best. And that makes sense: if your pencil factory keeps churning out broken pencils, you don't blame the pencils. You figure out what you can fine-tune on the factory floor. You improve the process to improve the things that the process creates.

That's what this chapter is about.

CREATIVITY IS DISCOVERY

Don't take this personally, but your next song isn't just about you. You might be the person who creates it, puts their name on it and says cool and intriguing things about it in a *Rolling Stone* interview. But slow down, punk, this is about your song too. From time to time your song is going to tell you what it wants and needs. It's your job to shut up and listen out for that.

The thing is, a work of art is its own kind of living organism. And like any living, breathing, functioning thing, the parts all have to be in their proper places for the whole thing to work properly. You could go all Dr Frankenstein and swap a person's brain and kidneys around, and as interesting an experiment as it might be, you'd quickly realize that a human body doesn't really work if you do that.

Songwriting works the same way. Sure, it's a creative act. But a creative act is also an act of discovery. You decide to write an uplifting ballad, so that affects the tempo or title you choose. You decide to make the first chord C major, so that affects what you choose for the second chord. You're making some choices and trying to discover what other choices go well with them. That's why there are no right and wrong creative choices – only choices that work well together.

Some people describe this process as pulling a song out of the air or out of the ether. It's as if the song already exists, you're just trying to uncover it. It's as if the statue is already in the block of marble, you just have to dig it out.

The big decision – the part where you're 100% holding the reigns – is when you decide what your song is or is about. What you might call the big vision. After that, you're trying to figure out the clearest or most interesting or most personal way of realizing that vision. And that's a process of trial and error, a process of discovery.

Yes, this might sound scary. It might sound like you're letting go of control exactly when you should be doing the opposite. But once you embrace this, you might be surprised by how liberating it is. Seriously, try it sometime. You'll become a medium or channel instead of a dictator. You'll stop trying to micro-manage every part of what you create and you'll let what you're creating lead you on a crazy adventure. Trust me, it's a lot more fun that way.

DISCOVERY MEANS DRAFTING

A big part of the process of discovery is discovering things that *don't* work. Because discovering things that don't work is a one of the best ways to discover the things that do.

That's just how it is. In life and art you have to make a lot of wrong turns before you can start making the right ones. In songwriting you usually have to write the half-assed version of something before you can write the fully-assed version. Sometimes it takes five, ten or twenty slightly different but still half-assed versions of a line or melody before you come up with one you really like. Sometimes it takes even more.

As they say: great songs aren't written, they're rewritten.

In fact, the more a work of art looks like it came out perfectly formed in some giant explosion of perfect inspiration, usually the more blood, sweat and tears that went into making it look that way. Plenty of great works of art weren't that great at some point in their creation – google 'dodgy early demos of classic songs' and you'll see what I mean.

Sure, it's easy and tempting to assume that great artists are just better at coming up with great ideas than everyone else, but it's just not true.

As any great artist will tell you, they come up with plenty of terrible ideas too. The only difference is that great artists have learned to be pickier. They don't settle for OK. They come up with as many ideas as they can and only roll with the best ones, or they just keep refining and improving the OK ideas until they become the best ones.

CREATIVITY IS INTUITIVE

One of the best things about creativity is that it's not always logical. Sometimes you come across a great work of art but you can't really explain why it's so great. It just works. Every part of it just somehow works together.

Part of the trick of drafting is sifting through all of the ideas in front of you and figuring out what to do with them. And often you'll start to see how some of this material might work well together. It's like a sports team line up where some of the ideas are whispering 'pick me, pick me!' just a bit louder than the others. Bit by bit, all of these ideas start to coalesce into a single whole.

But here's the weirdest thing: often you won't know why. You won't necessarily understand why one idea seems to go with some other idea. Sometimes as you revise something you'll find better and better ways to put two ideas together. You might not understand why one way is better than the other. But somehow you just know it's what your song needs. OK, you might look back in a year and it'll be obvious why you did it. But while you're in there creating, don't be surprised if sometimes you're riding on your intuition and not much else.

When it comes to making creative decisions, your gut knows things your rational brain can't put into words. You have to learn to trust that.

NO IDEAS ARE NEW

Your brain churns out new ideas, and you turn those new ideas into songs. But have you ever wondered where those ideas come from?

It turns out the answer is really simple and really interesting: new ideas are made of old ideas. New ideas are just old ideas dressed up differently or mixed up in new ways.

That means, in a sense, there are no new ideas. It means, in a sense, all art is made by stealing ideas from other art. As T. S. Eliot said, "Immature poets imitate;

mature poets steal; bad poets deface what they take, and good poets make it into something better, or at least something different."

This is exciting because it doesn't just give you permission to steal liberally from the art and artists you love, it means stealing from the art and artists you love is the only way to create something new. It means you have to drown in the ocean of influence before you can come up to the surface with something new and exciting.

But let's be clear, creativity isn't plagiarism. Creative theft doesn't mean copying someone else word for word or note for note. Sure, you can steal whatever you like, but you have to give as much as you take. You have to do something new with the things you steal. You have to take parts of some random thing you love and mix them together with parts of other random things you love. And that's called being original. That's called making something new.

"I wanted to hear music that had not yet happened, by putting together things that suggested a new thing which did not yet exist."

BRIAN ENO

Every artist wants to create something new. There's not much point in being an artist if you don't. But no one is going to reinvent their art form overnight. You have to be influenced. You have to take other people's ideas and do other things with them. You have to work with what's already out there and nudge it somewhere just new enough that it becomes original.

One way or another, everything you write is a love letter to the art you admire. And that's how it should be.

FIND A PROCESS THAT WORKS FOR YOU

Oh, and if you were wondering, there is no 'The Creative Process' or 'The Writing Process'. There's no single universal way everybody who makes new things has to do it. It's up to you to try things out and see what works well for you.

Maybe you usually start a song by working out the melody. Maybe you usually start by brainstorming lyric ideas on a blank page. Maybe you work best in two-hour chunks with strict fifteen-minute breaks. Maybe you create best with your laptop in a noisy café, or maybe you need your quiet space at home. Maybe you work best sketching out ideas by hand before you tidy things up on a screen somewhere. Maybe you need half an hour tidying your workspace, ironing your bed sheets or vacuuming the shower before your brain is settled enough to start creating properly. (Don't knock procrastination, by the way – it's where I get some of my best thinking done.)

But most of all: be ready to let your creative process take you somewhere new every time. However you do it, a work of art is created bit by bit and piece by piece. A work of art is hundreds or thousands of individual decisions that somehow all add up to one bigger thing. There are billions of different ways to end up with that one bigger thing.

And that, by the way, is the main reason I don't believe in writers' block. Sure, sometimes you sit down to write and it gushes forth like the Amazon. Sometimes it trickles out more like a leaky water bottle you bought on Amazon. But a trickle isn't a block. And, more importantly, that trickle might turn into a gush if you try a different route. You might not be able to write the chorus yet, but you might be able to write the first verse. Or you might be able to write the chorus if you go back a step and figure out some of the big picture questions we talked about in Chapter 4. Or riff on some chords the chorus might use. Or just try write a crappy chorus you know you'll improve later. Writer's block usually only exists because you aren't ready to create something you've told yourself you should be.

If something feels like a step forward, no matter how small, let it happen. Don't be afraid of trying new ways to get where you're trying to go. Don't feel discouraged if an idea doesn't come easily the first time you ask it to. Creativity doesn't always do what you ask it to. That's what makes it so exciting.

HOW TO BE INTERESTING

If creativity is about putting existing things together in new ways, creating something new is the art of putting things that don't usually go together together.

In fact, the more interesting and extraordinary the combination of things you put together, the more interesting and extraordinary the result overall.

Any old anyone can combine existing things in tried-and-tested ways. Any old anyone can use the same three chords that everyone uses, the same old lyrical clichés and all the obvious and predictable ways to say 'I love you'. But not everyone is bold and interesting enough to try new sounds, find an original way of saying something or just take a familiar idea and give it a twist nobody has before.

Which kind of person do you want to be?

And yes, doing something untested might make you feel nervous. You're taking a chance on something new and it might feel weird because you have no idea where you're heading. But you have to get used to that. You have to get used to going on bold and unexpected journeys, because once you do, there's every chance other people will want to come along with you. But only if you decide to go somewhere we can't go already.

Some great ideas sound really terrible at first. Who wants to listen to a six-minute opera-meets-pop song that nobody's really sure what it's about? Plenty of people, as it turned out. People love 'Bohemian Rhapsody' precisely because it's different. OK, you couldn't put out an album of twelve Bohemian Rhapsodies because then each track wouldn't be that different and wouldn't be that interesting. But every once in a while pursuing an idea that excites you but seems random, weird or stupid at first is a great way of creating something really original.

CREATIVITY TAKES COURAGE

It takes courage to take big risks on bold ideas. It takes courage to keep going when you have no idea how things might turn out. It takes courage to keep figuring things out as you go along. That's what makes being creative so challenging. But it's also what makes being creative so exciting.

It can be scary to take big risks. But if you want to be really good at making exciting, new things, you don't have much choice. Taking a big risk might mean you end up with something terrible, but as it turns out, taking a big risk is the only way to end up with something really great. Incredible, unexpected and life-changing things only come from risky places.

Of course, you can always play it safe. You can always shoot for a four, five or six out of ten. Though then you've kind of lost by default. But otherwise, if you want to risk making something that's a seven, you have to take a chance it'll end up a three. If you want an eight, you have to take a chance it'll end up a two. And if you want to blow us away with a nine or ten, well, you get the idea.

But here's the other thing: the best part about taking risks is that every time you risk something, you're rewarded. Maybe not in the way you expected, maybe not in any way you could have imagined. But every risk is rewarded all the same – maybe with new knowledge, new experience, new confidence, or something else entirely. Try it and see.

Being creative means adjusting your definition of success to include trying hard and taking risks, whatever the result. It means accepting risk as a necessary part of trying to do new and exciting things. It means understanding that taking risks doesn't always work out in the short term, but as a long-game strategy it's one of the most powerful tools you've got.

The good news is finding the courage to do that is pretty simple. Courage is just like a muscle: the more you use it the more it grows. You've just got to keep chipping away at your comfort zone and training yourself to be more comfortable being uncomfortable. You've just got to learn to feel the fear but decide to push ahead anyway.

In other words, it's not that the challenge gets any less challenging. It's just that you get better at rising to it.

FUNDAMENTAL SONGWRITING CHALLENGE #5

Prime your creative brain to let it make magic at its best.

[6]

STRUCTURE

"If I'm never tied to anything, I'll never be free."
STEPHEN SCHWARTZ, *Pippin*

WHAT IS STRUCTURE?

Structure, or form, is what gives your song shape and direction. It's the scaffolding your song hangs its ideas on. It's the circus tent where your song performs its tricks.

And a song with no structure is just an amorphous blob. Like Celine Dion's heart, it just seems to go on and on and on.

In songwriting, a solid structure means having a plan for how a song's various sections repeat and fit together. It means finding a nice balance between unity – things that are similar – and variety – things that aren't – so that everything in your song feels like it belongs together but doesn't feel too repetitive.

And just like a novel is made up of words that form sentences, sentences that form paragraphs, paragraphs that form sections, and sections that form chapters, a song is made by adding parts together too, though usually in a much simpler way. In a song, words come together to form lines (while individual notes form the musical phrases that go with them) and those lines come together to form sections. As a rough guide, let's say your typical song has five to twelve sections, each made up of maybe four to sixteen lines.

What gives each section its own identity is what everything within that section has in common. The things that go into a verse tend to do a slightly different job to the things that tend to go into a chorus, for example. In fact, a big part of understanding how structure works is understanding what each part of a song is supposed to do, so that you can take all the ideas that could go into the song and lasso the verse-like ideas into the verses, the chorus-like ideas into the choruses, and so on.

But the point of putting material that does verse-like things and chorus-like things together to create different sections is so that those sections can work together to do something each individual section couldn't do on its own. Each section has its own purpose that plays some specific part within the bigger structure of your song. That's the central idea of creating a solid song structure.

FUNDAMENTAL SONGWRITING CHALLENGE #6

Create a song structure made up of individual sections that fit together to form a single, unified whole.

So those are some key structure principles in a nutshell, and there are all kinds of ways to apply them in practice. We'll start by looking at one of the most common – verse-chorus structures – which we'll then use as a gateway drug to talking about two slightly more hardcore but also fairly common structures – refrain forms and 32-bar forms.

VERSE-CHORUS STRUCTURES

As a ballpark figure, verse-chorus structures make up something like 90% of songs written today, or at least 90% of the songs you find in the charts. That doesn't mean this type of structure is automatically better than any other, but it does mean it's a type of structure worth knowing about, whatever kind of music you want to create.

One of the reasons verse-chorus structures are so great – and so common – is that there are lots of different ways to make a good one, based on a few common patterns and a handful of fundamental ideas. That means this isn't going to be a painting-by-numbers guide to structuring a verse-chorus song. Instead, we're going to go on a tour of the common building blocks that make up verse-chorus structures. We'll talk about what these sections do, why and how they do it, and how you can go about making these blocks work together in a song.

THE VERSE-CHORUS CYCLE

It's probably no surprise to you that the two most important sections in a verse-chorus structure – and the only two that aren't really optional – are the verse and the chorus.

You'll usually find verses and choruses in pairs – but they're not quite equal pairs. The verse is the warm up act that gets us ready for the chorus to be the headliner. The verse is the wingman who sets the chorus up to score. In other words, the verse's job is to set up and build into the chorus, and the chorus's job is to get right to the heart of what your song is trying to say.

That's why I call the two sections together a cycle. When they're working well together, there's a definite sense of forward motion as you go from verse to chorus. And getting to the next verse feels like starting over somehow.

The verses set up the song by providing background information in the lyric and establishing the song's groove – the core instrumental feel that characterizes the song – in the music. And because a verse's job is to anticipate the chorus, they often feel like they're moving somewhere new at some point in the second half as they get closer to the chorus. This often means the lyric starts to go in a slightly different direction, or the harmony becomes more adventurous, or the texture – the number of instrumental parts involved and how busy those parts are – starts to build. Often it's a combination of all three.

The chorus is the focal point of your song. It's where you say what your song is about most directly. It's pretty much always where you put your song's hook – a repeated word or phrase that forms the spine of your song's lyric. (We'll talk about what this means in more detail in a couple of chapters' time.) Musically, a chorus is usually more intense than the verse before it: the rhythms are often more energetic, the vocal melody might be in a slightly higher register, and the texture tends to be thicker and busier. As a general principle, you want your choruses to draw more attention to themselves than your verses do.

Repeated verse-chorus cycles form the backbone of a verse-chorus structure. There are often two or three cycles, and sometimes even four or five. This is what three looks like:

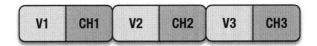

Sometimes the chorus is repeated an extra time (or a couple of times) at the end too:

Let's see this in action in a straightforward example. Here are the first two verse-chorus cycles of Tom Jones's 'Delilah', by Les Reed and Barry Mason:

VERSE   I saw the light on the night that I passed by her window.

I saw the flickering shadow of love on her blind.

She was my woman.

As she deceived me I watched and went out of my mind.

CHORUS My, my, my, Delilah.

Why, why, why, Delilah?

I could see, that girl was no good for me,

But I was lost like a slave that no man could free.

VERSE   At break of day when that man drove away I was waiting.

I crossed the street to her house and she opened the door.

She stood there laughing.

I felt the knife in my hand and she laughed no more.

CHORUS My, my, my, Delilah.

Why, why, why, Delilah?

So before they come to break down the door.

Forgive me Delilah I just couldn't take any more.

So you'll see the basic idea that the verses set the scene and start telling the song's story – we get the details about what Delilah did to drive this guy crazy, and we see how he responds – and the choruses hammer home the song's central idea – that Delilah drove this guy crazy.

'Delilah' is also a great example of some other things that are typical of how verse-chorus structures work.

First of all, you'll probably know the basic idea that the verses use the same (or nearly the same) music but with different lyrics, which if you listen, you'll hear

'Delilah' does. This practice is pretty much the standard – you want the chorus to stay pretty static and familiar, and the verses to move things forward. Still, it's common to make minor changes to the verse's melody to accommodate places where there's a syllable or two extra (or missing) between verses. (If you look closely at the last lines of each verse in 'Delilah' you'll see what I mean.)

'Delilah' is also a great example of the verses talking about different things and helping to continue the story – you'll see the second verse goes from night to the next day, and from this guy watching Delilah getting busy with someone else to him standing at her front door and stabbing her. We'll talk about more ways to do that – plan out your verses, not kill people – in Chapter 9.

Second of all, you'll probably also know that in a verse-chorus structure the choruses usually have the same music and the same lyric each time – or at least, a similar lyric each time. 'Delilah' happens to fall in the similar lyric category: the last two lines of each chorus are different. That's not uncommon, and when it happens it's usual for the lyric to change somewhere in the middle or near the end – as 'Delilah' does – so you still get the feeling of arriving at the chorus whenever it comes back. That's important because you want your chorus to feel like a familiar landing point each time you take us back there.

Finally, 'Delilah' is a great example of how you generally want your verses and choruses to be a similar length. At least, it's rare to find verses that are way longer than the chorus: as the saying goes, 'Don't bore us, get to the chorus'.

You could write an entire book about section lengths in songwriting, but as a general principle, it's common for each line of lyric to be one or two measures of music. ('Delilah' has eight measures per lyric line, so this is absolutely, definitively not a rule.) But if you're not sure where to start, four or eight lines (and the same or double the number of measures) for each verse and chorus is a great length to try.

That said, as you get more practice you should know about a common technique where you make the second verse (and third verse, if there is one) to be half the length of the first. This usually means creating your first verse out of two identical (or nearly identical) halves, but only using one of them in later verses. To see what this looks like in practice, you can check out Jason Mraz's 'Hello, You Beautiful Thing' and Bette Middler's 'Wind Beneath My Wings'.

THE BRIDGE

After verse and chorus, the third most important section in verse-chorus structures is the bridge. (You might also hear it called the release, the middle eight or the primary bridge.)

The bridge stands out from the other sections around it by being totally different from them. In fact, that's kind of the point of a bridge: to take us somewhere we haven't been already. The melody and harmonies are usually brand new, the instrumental texture is different to anything in the song so far, and the lyric usually goes somewhere totally new too.

The most common place to put the bridge is after the second chorus, like this:

In fact, this structure – two verse-chorus cycles, a bridge, a final chorus – is pretty much the archetypal verse-chorus structure. I promised I wouldn't give you a formula to copy, but if you're new to songwriting and want a structure to take out of the box, this is a great place to start: just try to make each section four or eight lines long and get writing.

In this archetypal structure, you'll see the bridge essentially replaces the third verse. But from time to time you also get a third verse after the bridge for good measure:

In these cases, it's not uncommon to reuse part or all of one of the other verse's lyric in the third verse. You sometimes also find that the third verse is a cut-down or somehow altered verse to keep the momentum going.

With or without that extra verse, the place where the bridge usually goes isn't just coincidental. You'll see it comes at exactly the moment that repeating the verse-chorus cycle over and over would start to get predictable: you hear it twice through so you might expect it a third time, but the bridge throws a spanner in the works and sends the song in a fresh, unexpected direction.

And this idea is at the heart of creating a great bridge: a sense of departure, diversion or escape. (Check out virtually any song with a bridge and you'll start to see the millions of ways you can do this in practice.)

Lyrically, this usually means talking about something related to the song's big idea but something you haven't talked about yet. Sometimes a bridge flashes forwards or backwards in time. Sometimes they add a bigger perspective or broader context to your song. Whatever they do, a good bridge is a one-way street: we come out of the other side seeing the song's message in a different light.

A really clear-cut example of this is Katy Perry's 'I Kissed a Girl'. The bridge adds a new and more philosophical perspective: 'Ain't no big deal, it's innocent'. There's a definite feeling of coming out the other side understanding the song's message in a broader or more nuanced way.

Musically, bridges are also a departure. They usually go somewhere that feels strange and new, ready to return us back to the solid ground of the final chorus or choruses. If the verse is about anticipating and leading into the chorus, the bridge is more about escaping from it.

One common way of doing this is to give a bridge a thinner texture – maybe by having the bass or drums drop out – so that when the final chorus comes back with a fuller texture, the sense of return is much stronger because of the contrast immediately before it. ('I Kissed a Girl' is also a great example of this. Check it out.)

THE PRE-CHORUS

I've already mentioned how it's common for verses to start moving in a new direction as they get close to the chorus. This is one way of accentuating the rise and fall that's an essential part of a verse-chorus cycle.

But sometimes, this function goes to a section in its own right: a linking section between verse and chorus called the pre-chorus. (You might also hear it called the climb or transitional bridge.)

In a nutshell, the pre-chorus makes a bigger deal out of this build than a verse might on its own, giving the verse-chorus cycle three distinct sections, like this:

Sometimes the pre-chorus also comes back before the final chorus, like this:

(If you really like living on the edge, you can even bring back the verse *and* pre-chorus before the third chorus. Though this happens rarely enough I'm not going to give you a diagram.)

As you can see in the diagrams I have given you, including a pre-chorus once pretty much commits you to doing it in all of the other complete verse-chorus cycles. Musically, just like the other sections, each time a pre-chorus comes back it's based on the same material, maybe with minor changes. Lyrically, pre-choruses can be anywhere from different every time (like verses usually are) or identical every time (like choruses usually are). But in practice they're often somewhere in the middle, made of a combination of identical and different lyric lines.

There are all kinds of lengths you can make your pre-chorus. One common technique is to make the verse and pre-chorus equal in length, then make the chorus the length of the two combined – so your verse and pre-chorus might be four lines each, and your chorus eight lines. But it's not uncommon to find verses of, say, eight lines followed by a pre-chorus of four or two lines, then a chorus of eight. As usual, the best way to figure all of this out is to take apart as many songs with pre-choruses as you can – though if there's one general principle to bear in mind, it's that you don't want your pre-chorus to be significantly longer than your verse.

To talk in a bit more detail about how a pre-chorus works, let's look at the first verse-chorus cycle of Train's 'Drive By', by Pat Monahan, Espen Lind and Amund Bjørkland:

> VERSE   On the other side of a street I knew,
> Stood a girl that looked like you.
> I guess that's déjà vu
> But I thought this can't be true,
> 'Cause you moved to West LA,
> Or New York or Santa Fe,
> Or wherever to get away
> From me.
>
> PRE-CH   Oh, but that one night
> Was more than just right.
> I didn't leave you
> 'Cause I was all through.
> Oh, I was overwhelmed
> And frankly scared as hell,
> Because I really fell
> For you.
>
> CHORUS   Oh, I swear to ya,
> I'll be there for ya.

This is not a drive by-y-y-y-y.

Just a shy guy

Looking for a two-ply

Hefty bag to hold my-y-y-y-y-y love.

When you move me

Everything is groovy.

They don't like it sue me,

Mmm, the way you do me.

Oh, I swear to ya,

I'll be there for ya.

This is not a drive by-y-y-y.

The verse and the chorus do pretty much what we saw in 'Delilah': the verse starts telling the story – about a girl who left town, leaving this guy behind – and the chorus hammers home the central idea – that this guy is in it for the long haul. But the pre-chorus adds an extra layer in between. It makes a leap in a new direction – talking about some night they shared together and him admitting he freaked out because he'd fallen for her. The pre-chorus tells us something new, adds an extra dimension to the story and starts moving things towards the chorus.

And that's pretty much what pre-choruses do. Despite the name, a pre-chorus is normally more an extension or development of the verse than a precursor to the chorus. It's the catalyst that starts a subtle but distinctive turn towards the chorus. Just like a chorus builds on a verse in a two-part cycle, in a three-part cycle each section builds on the one before, upping the ante towards the moment the chorus lands. And this is the central skill of writing a pre-chorus: finding a way to make a verse, pre-chorus and chorus function as a trio.

In practice, there are lots of ways you can do this. Often, you discover a neat way of doing it as you write. But if in doubt, here's a good template to know about:

Verse	Well…
Pre-chorus	But…
Chorus	So…

In short, you use your verse to set the scene with a 'Well…' thought. You flip things around a bit in the pre-chorus with a 'But…' thought. Then you use that to get to your big 'So…' point in your chorus. Like in this outline I just made up:

Verse	Well, things have been great recently.
Pre-chorus	But the past few days you've been distant.
Chorus	So are you going to tell me what's going on?

It works because each idea flows neatly into the next one. It works because the progression is logical. You don't even need to include the 'well', 'but' or 'so' – if the meaning is there, it'll work. And like we talked about at the start of the chapter, each section has its own identity (each says something different to any of the other sections) but they all add up to say something bigger overall.

All you'd have to do in a real song is expand these one-line summaries into full lyrics that fill a section. And when it comes to writing your second verse-chorus cycle, just like in a two-part cycle, you'd just have to find different details to flesh out the same or similar ideas a second time. Though, as a reminder, often the lyrics to the pre-chorus are similar or identical each time, so you might not need to come up different words every time it comes back.

As usual, this template isn't the only way you can make a pre-chorus work. In general, it's really effective to connect sections with a conceptual 'but' or 'so' – you might be surprised how many bridges, choruses and pre-choruses in particular work this way – but there's no reason you can't do the same thing with an 'and' thought, or an 'anyway' thought, or a much looser connection that you can't categorize as neatly as this. Still, the well-but-so template is a good one to know about if you're not sure where to start with pre-choruses and want something definite to work with. (Incidentally, 'Drive By' is pretty much a well-but-so structure too – there's a red-herring 'but' in the first verse that doesn't kick off a new thought, but the core concept is there. See if you can spot how.)

So if that's what pre-choruses do lyrically, musically they do similar things to what the end of a verse usually does: building in intensity, going new places harmonically and growing in texture. Though unlike in a verse, you'll often find these things start to happen fairly suddenly to mark the beginning of the pre-chorus – if you listen to 'Drive By' you'll hear the drums get heavier and an extra keyboard layer appear in the texture subtly but suddenly at 'Oh, but that one night'.

That said, sometimes the difference musically between the verse and pre-chorus is more subtle than sudden. So much so you might wonder whether a song has a verse and pre-chorus or just a big verse that builds towards the end. And the good news is the answer doesn't really matter. Often you could argue the case either way. And that's all good. What counts is the way the song builds into the chorus, not the way you label it.

For another song with a clear-cut pre-chorus you can check out Oasis's 'Wonderwall'. (The pre-chorus is from 'All the roads that lead us there...'.) And for a song where it's up for debate whether it's a verse that starts to build or a verse and distinct pre-chorus, you can check out Bruno Mars's 'Grenade'.

INTROS AND OUTROS

We've now covered the four principal sections that make up a verse-chorus structure. So let's take a look at a few of the other sections you can use to mix a verse-chorus structure up a bit.

Lots of songs include an intro before the first verse, like this:

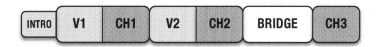

An intro's job is to set up the song's groove before the vocal comes in properly at the beginning of the first verse. Sometimes an intro features small chunks of the main lyric, or some vocal riffing, or a spoken introduction from the singer, but usually the lyric doesn't start properly until the first verse.

Some intros are made out of totally distinctive material, though often an intro is derived from musical material elsewhere in the song. Very often, an intro is just the verse's groove without the vocal on top. ('Drive By' is also a great example of this.)

It's also common to use the chorus or part of the chorus as an intro. If so, the chorus often appears in a kind of thinned-out preview or teaser form, where the texture or vocal is reduced somehow. This is a great way to plant the chorus in your audience's brains before you get there for real. (Check out Cee Lo Green's 'Forget You' for a good example of this technique in action.)

Generally, it's a good idea to keep your intro short. Don't bore us, get to the chorus, right? Most intros are maybe two, four or eight measures. Longer intros are definitely possible – the full version of The Buggles's 'Video Killed the Radio Star' makes a feature of a much longer intro that isn't copied and pasted from elsewhere in the song, and Michael Jackson's 'Thriller' has a long intro which eventually morphs into the verse groove. But it's worth mentioning that the radio edits of both of these songs keep the intro nice and short.

If the intro goes at the start of your song, it's probably no surprise that an outro – or ending – comes at the end:

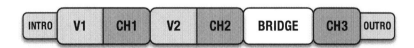

Just like with intros, an outro is usually derived from somewhere else in the song. Sometimes the last chorus is extended with a short ending of a measure or two. Sometimes the outro is just the chorus an extra time as a repeat-and-fade. Occasionally the outro is derived from the intro. As usual, keep your ears out for how the outros work in your favorite songs. There are all kinds of possibilities.

INSTRUMENTALS

Instrumental sections do what they say on the tin: the vocal drops out to make a feature of the music for a few measures – often for an instrumental solo on guitar, sax, drums or whatever performer you want to showcase.

An instrumental often replaces the bridge, though sometimes there's a vocal bridge as well, either before or after:

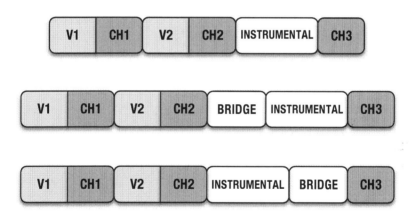

You can also create all kinds of hybrid versions, where there's some vocal going on but the music really comes to the fore like in an ordinary instrumental. Jennifer Lopez's 'Waiting for Tonight' is a good example of this – the bridge features some sultry vocal riffing with a trumpet solo going on at the same time. Look out for some more unusual ways instrumentals can work in the songs you love.

TAGS: TURNAROUNDS, POST-CHORUSES AND DROPS

It's common to find a short (or short-ish) section after a song's chorus, for a handful of different reasons. There's no more-or-less universal term for these, but I'm going to call them tags, and let's take a look at three common functions they can perform.

Sometimes a tag is just a quick breather – of maybe two or four measures – for both your singer and the audience. These types of tags are often called turnarounds.

Turnarounds are often made up of the chorus groove chugging away for a few more measures, maybe with a short instrumental solo or a bit of vocal riffing over the top. Their point is to offer a quick break before the song moves somewhere new. You can check out Dolly Parton's '9 to 5' for a good example: after each chorus there's a two-measure interlude from the band before the next verse starts.

Sometimes a tag is used to hammer home the chorus's big idea a bit more than normal, as a kind of extension of the chorus proper. These sections are especially common in commercial pop music, they often last eight or so measures, and they're usually called post-choruses.

Post-choruses are often made up of material related to the chorus and often feature the hook repeated over and over, maybe between 'yeah's and 'ooh's or something like that. It's a way of giving the audience at least a bit of a breather – as there's no new information in a post-chorus – as well as ensuring your hook is planted in your audience's brains a few extra times. Check out Beyoncé's 'Love on Top' for a great example of this in action.

Sometimes though, a tag actually outdoes the chorus. This type of tag – usually called a drop – is especially common in more recent dance music. Like with a pre-chorus, they essentially split the chorus-y bit of your song into two parts, except unlike with a pre-chorus, the drop is the section where the song really hits *instead* of the chorus. So instead of having a verse build into a big chorus you essentially get a verse building into a chorus building into a drop – or even a verse that builds and then a chorus that pulls back to let the drop really hit.

That means that with a drop, the chorus does what a chorus usually does lyrically – it has the main idea of the song in it, it's where the hook goes – it just doesn't quite pop musically like a traditional chorus does, saving that for the drop. And while drops often feature a word or line of the lyric, the most important thing about them is their music – they're usually about creating a big dance section within the verse-chorus cycle.

If that sounds complicated, go check out Timeflies's 'Once in a While' for a great example of this in practice. You'll hear how the chorus is where the hook goes but musically it pulls back so the drop – which doesn't have a full-on lyric but repeats 'I feel good' a few times – can be the main event.

So while all of these types of sections – turnarounds, post-choruses and drops – might come in the same spot after the chorus, they're there to do subtly different things. Turnarounds are there to give us a breather. Post-choruses are there to give us the chorus's message an extra bit. And drops are usually there to make us put our hands in the air like we just don't care.

This also means these different types of tag affect where and how the verse-chorus cycle peaks in intensity. I've tried to represent that in the diagrams this time by shading them in more detail to show how they typically rise and fall – darker color means more intensity:

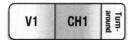 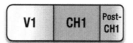 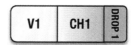

Can you see the difference? Turnarounds make space for a timeout between cycles. Post-choruses extend the high of the chorus. And drops make the drop the big high and the chorus the anticipation instead. Same basic rise and fall, just subtly different ways of making it happen.

Obviously, and as always, this shading is just a representation and not a strict decree. As usual, it's your job to keep an eye out for how different types of tags work in the genre or genres you want to write in. Plus, when you get down to the level of detail we're talking about with tags, trends and common practices can change relatively quickly – by the time you're reading this there might other popular ways of using tags in the verse-chorus cycle. This is just another demonstration that though the central idea of a verse-chorus cycle's rise and fall is pretty much universal, there are lots of ways to make it happen in practice.

Finally, I kept pre-choruses out of this section for simplicity, but in case you were wondering, yes, it is possible to include a pre-chorus and a tag in a single verse-chorus cycle. That said, you're much more likely to find a dedicated pre-chorus when the tag is a turnaround or a pre-chorus, since including a drop usually means the chorus is the big climb, so a pre-chorus would probably be redundant.

THE BIG TABLE

So by now we've covered all the usual sections that go into verse-chorus structures. And if you're the kind of person who loves having that sort of stuff all summarized in a big table you can refer back to – I have good news. I made one.

Turn your head sideways and see what you think:

OPENING	VERSE–CHORUS CYCLES				CONTRAST	RETURN	
Sets up groove and world of song.	Alternating VERSES and CHORUSES. VERSES set up and build into CHORUSES. Later cycles often varied in subtle or profound ways.				Something new and diversionary.	Final arrival at CHORUS plus conclusion of song.	
INTRO	**VERSE 1**	**CHORUS 1**	**VERSE 2**	**CHORUS 2**	**BRIDGE**	**CHORUS 3**	**OUTRO**
INTRO • No proper lyric yet, but maybe vocal riffing • May be derived from VERSE or CHORUS and/or **CHORUS** • In full or part • Often a 'preview' version, thinned out or altered somehow	**VERSE** • Basic groove • Sets up background to song • Around half-way point, often starts to build noticeably in anticipation of CHORUS and sometimes **PRE-CHORUS** • Distinct transitional section • Marked change in lyric direction, harmony or texture as moves towards CHORUS	**CHORUS** • States central idea of song • Most memorable section • Bigger groove, thickest texture or most energy so far and sometimes **TAG** • Maybe gives singer a break with short TURNAROUND, maybe extends CHORUS with POST-CHORUS, or outdoes CHORUS with even bigger DROP	**VERSE** • Shares more background info or detail • Almost always new lyric • May be shorter than VERSE 1 (often half the length) and sometimes **PRE-CHORUS** • Same effect as PRE-CHORUS 1 • Lyric is often identical or very similar to PRE-CHORUS 1	**CHORUS** • Lyric usually identical to CHORUS 1, maybe with minor changes • Sometimes changes in texture to CHORUS 1 and sometimes **TAG** • Same effect as TAG 1 • Texture sometimes changed	Various possibilities: **BRIDGE** • Totally distinct from anything so far • Lyric adds a new perspective and/or **INSTRUMENTAL** Vocal drops out for instrumental solo or maybe dance section and sometimes then **VERSE** or **PRE-CHORUS** or **VERSE & PRE-CHORUS** • Links BRIDGE and final CHORUS • Texture, lyric or length may be altered	**CHORUS** • CHORUS may be repeated • Often something new in instrumental texture, or major vocal riffing added • Lyric usually identical to other CHORUSES, though sometimes minor changes • Final CHORUS often the biggest moment in the song	**SUDDEN STOP** or **REPEAT & FADE** • Chorus repeated and fades out or **OUTRO** • Distinct ending • No proper lyric, though maybe vocal riffing • May be totally new but often derived from CHORUS, VERSE or INTRO

CREATING A VERSE-CHORUS STRUCTURE THAT WORKS

So that's our magical mystery tour of the common components you can use to build a verse-chorus structure. But with so many different options and permutations, how do you go about finding the right verse-chorus structure for your next song?

Well, as you know, there's no such thing as the definitive right one. There are all kinds of verse-chorus structures you can build that work well, and that's kind of the fun.

But at the same time, here's an important principle that might help guide you: content dictates form.

That means you're trying to find a structure that lets your song say what it needs to say in the way you want it to say it. You don't just pick a structure and pour ideas into it. You figure out what your content is and let that guide your song's structure.

We looked at how you can create an effective bridge, but in real life sometimes you'll find you're not sure what to put in one – which means you probably don't need it. This is content dictating form. And the same idea applies with all of the other sections. If your song needs to crash in and get moving right away, don't include an intro. If you don't need much of a dedicated build into your chorus, or you can't figure out what to put in a pre-chorus, don't include one. You get the idea.

In a good structure, content dictates form because you don't want any redundant sections. You don't want any parts that don't really belong or don't help you say what your song is trying to say. There's nothing wrong with writing a simple structure if that's what your song needs. And there's definitely nothing wrong with writing a simple structure if you're not ready to try something more adventurous just yet.

Feel free to adventure just as much as you need to, and as much as your song wants you to. Often you'll try out a version of a structure and realize your song doesn't quite work with it. So you might cut the pre-chorus or see if it works as a bridge or see if some of those ideas can go in your second verse instead. That's how it works. As you get more proficient with verse-chorus structures, you might find yourself doing all kinds of crazy and unorthodox things. As long as it ends up with the sections it needs to say what it has to say, it's all good.

As always, you've got to listen to what your song needs. You've got to let it take you where it wants to go. And in a nutshell, that's how content dictates form.

REFRAIN FORMS

Looking at verse-chorus structures is a great way to see some of the fundamental ideas that go into crafting a song's structure in action. But next, let's look at refrain forms, a different but related way of using these ideas.

Essentially, refrain forms compress the verse-chorus cycle into a single section, which is usually just called a verse. That means each verse or each cycle finishes with the same one or two lines. These lines are called the refrain.

A refrain is different from a chorus in two important ways. One: a refrain is much shorter than a chorus, and two: there's less of a distinction between what is the refrain and what isn't. More often than not, the refrain seems to grow naturally out of the verse without making a big deal out of it. So each cycle feels like it's made out of one complete unit, rather than two or three parts joined together:

This will make more sense with an example. Here are three cycles of Leonard Cohen's 'Hallelujah':

> Well I've heard there was a secret chord,
> That David played and it pleased the Lord.
> But you don't really care for music, do ya?

Well it goes like this: the fourth, the fifth,

The minor fall and the major lift,

The baffled king composing hallelujah.

REFRAIN   Hallelujah, hallelujah,

                 Hallelujah, hallelujah.

Well your faith was strong but you needed proof.

You saw her bathing on the roof.

Her beauty and the moonlight overthrew ya.

She tied you to her kitchen chair,

And she broke your throne and she cut your hair,

And from your lips she drew the hallelujah.

REFRAIN   Hallelujah, hallelujah,

                 Hallelujah, hallelujah.

You say I took the name in vain.

I don't even know the name.

But if I did, well really, what's it to you?

There's a blaze of light in every word.

It doesn't matter which you heard,

The holy or the broken hallelujah.

REFRAIN   Hallelujah, hallelujah,

                 Hallelujah, hallelujah.

You'll see that those repeated 'hallelujah's work in a similar way to a chorus: they're a familiar idea the song keeps coming back to. But if you listen to the song you'll notice they blend pretty tidily into the rest of the section. Sure, they're a bit different to everything else around them, but they're not different enough musically to have an identity as an independent section. Call them the Puerto Rico, the Isle of Man, the Hong Kong of songwriting if you like.

But, like a chorus, you'll notice the refrain is identical each time it returns, and it's also where the hook goes. (Though in 'Hallelujah' you'll also see the hook in the main body of each verse, just before the refrain.)

The fun thing about refrain forms is that you can have virtually any number of verses. Three is pretty much the minimum, 'Hallelujah' has anywhere from three to five depending on whose version you listen to, and some folk songs have way more than that, even dozens. You can just keep churning them out as long as there's more of your song's story to tell.

That said, three is probably the most common number – you might also see refrain forms called AAA forms for that reason – and that's a great place to start if you're still getting to grips with the form.

Everything I said about intros, outros and instrumentals applies to refrain forms too, if you want to mix the basic pattern up a bit. That said, refrain forms generally keep things simpler, with maybe an intro and outro and not much else added.

Refrain forms are especially good for songs that tell a strong story, or tell a story in an especially direct way, because you can pack all of that information into the verses and the refrain is much less of an interruption than a full-on chorus. If the game in a verse-chorus structure is usually to get to the chorus, where the main event of your song is, in a refrain form it's often the other way round: the story you weave outside of the refrains is at least as important as what goes on inside the refrains.

For that reason, refrain forms are particularly common in folk and country music, and for two great examples you can check out Simon and Garfunkel's 'Bridge Over Troubled Water' and Bob Dylan's 'Blowin' in the Wind'. Both songs use the common pattern of three verses with two-line refrains.

32-BAR FORMS

32-bar forms, or AABA forms, are a different kind of compressed verse-chorus structure. They look like this:

Like in a refrain form, 32-bar forms pack the verse-chorus cycle into a single section, the A. That's where the hook usually goes, often as the section's first or last line.

Just like the bridge in a verse-chorus structure, the B comes after two As, just when things might start to get predictable. And just like a good bridge, the B section's job is to shoot off somewhere new, with different music and a different direction in the lyric.

This means that arriving at the final A is supposed to give you the sense of return you usually get going from a bridge into a final chorus. And similar to the way you can modify a final chorus, the final A section is often extended or altered somehow – which you might see notated as AABA'.

AABA forms often also include a verse, though just for the sake of keeping you on your toes, this kind of verse is a completely different thing to the verses in any of the structures we've talked about so far. In fact, this kind of verse is more like fairly substantial introduction that comes *before* the main AABA. Like this:

If the main idea of the song goes in the As (with some kind of twist or flip in the B), the verse is a sort of preamble that sets that up.

Here's George and Ira Gershwin's 'I Got Rhythm', which happens to be a textbook example, to show you how that works:

VERSE   Days can be sunny, with never a sigh;
        Don't need what money can buy.
        Birds in the trees sing their day full of song.
        Why shouldn't we sing along?
        I'm chipper all the day,
        Happy with my lot.
        How do I get that way?
        Look at what I've got:

A   I got rhythm,
        I got music,
        I got my girl –
        Who could ask for anything more?

A   I got daisies,
        In green pastures,
        I got my girl –
        Who could ask for anything more?

B   Ol' man trouble,
        I don't mind him –
        You won't find him
        'Round my door.

A   I got starlight,
        I got sweet dreams,
        I got my girl –

> Who could ask for anything more –
>
> Who could ask for anything more?

First let's talk about the main body of the AABA. You'll see how the A sections pretty much repeat the same main idea in three different ways – with a big list of cool things this guy's got – all with the same end-line, 'Who could ask for anything more?'. (You'll also see the final A is extended by repeating that line an extra time.) Meanwhile, the B mixes things up a bit by talking about the opposite – what this guy *hasn't* got. (This kind of opposite-flip is very common.)

The verse's job is to take us from a standing start to the song's big idea in a few lines. You'll see it does that, talking about that big idea without saying it directly, and ending with the great setup line 'Look at what I've got'.

32-bar forms were particularly popular in the first half of the twentieth century – most jazz standards are AABA forms. But the form is still used often today – especially in cabaret and theatre music, and occasionally in pop and rock ballads (almost always without a verse at the top). Because AABA forms tend to be relatively short, it's common either to repeat the complete AABA a few times, or to repeat just the last half to create an AABABA structure.

For other examples of 32-bar form, there's The Beatles's 'Yesterday' and Billy Joel's 'She's Always a Woman' – which are both AABABA structures with no verse.

ONE MORE THING: STRUCTURE ISN'T JUST BLOCKS

So far we've looked at structure as the building blocks that go together to give your song shape. And those blocks are important – they're at the core of how your structure works.

But there's a bit more to it than that. Creating an effective song structure isn't just about putting different blocks side by side. It's also about the journey you weave between those blocks and the relationships they have with each other – including blocks that aren't directly next to each other.

For example, are the textures in different choruses slightly different each time to create some kind of overall progression? Is the groove in each verse slightly different too? Do you kick off the bridge with a key change? Do you save the key change for the final chorus? Do you want the transition into the bridge to be gentle or sudden? Does some musical feature of the intro somehow make it into the chorus?

We've looked at a few questions like these in passing, but thinking about them in a bit more detail is part of mastering how song structures work. Balancing unity and variety means thinking about the web of little relationships that create similarities and differences throughout your song. It means thinking about a song in its entirety, as the sum of all of its many parts.

And that's important. If you make a Japanese garden, people can wander round as fast or as slow as they want and in whatever order they want. And that's kind of the point of a Japanese garden. But if you write a song, you get to make all of those decisions. You get to think about how people experience your song overall – how you take us from start to end, where the highs and lows are, and where you give us things we know already and where we get to be surprised by something new.

In short, you get to control of the journey your song takes us on. So use that power well, compadre. It's what creating solid song structures is all about.

So there are some of the ideas that go into making a song's structure work. Like I said way back in the introduction, now it's your job to see how these ideas apply to the songs you admire and see what you can learn from that.

You'll probably find some songs that follow these principles to the letter, and you'll probably find some that don't. And that's OK. That's how it's supposed to be. As usual, theory isn't always the same as practice. There are ideas and principles that help make structures work, but there are no rules.

As you get more experienced at writing you'll probably find yourself experimenting with different structures and even coming up with things that seem really wild and unorthodox. And if you feel ready for that already, that's great.

But if not, structure is one of the few areas where I strongly recommend you buckle down and master the plain, archetypal forms before you start to venture off-piste. Structure is such a central part of how songwriting works that it's not really a good idea to make up anything you like and just hope for the best.

Because here's the thing: if one or more of the songs you admire seems to have an unorthodox structure, I almost guarantee you the person who created it had written plenty of textbook structures before they started being more adventurous. And I almost guarantee you that those unorthodox structures are based on the same fundamental principles more regular structures are – only used in different ways, or selectively adapted to fit what a particular song needed.

So sure, if you've got a passion for adventure, don't lose it. Let it simmer away while you get a better grasp of how structure works. Because the more you write, and the better you understand these fundamental ideas, the better you'll understand which parts of them are negotiable and which definitely aren't. As always, that's the best way to make your own rules.

[7]

HOOKS

"A title is vital; Once you've it, prove it."

IRA GERSHWIN

Here's a really fundamental principle of life: the more you repeat something, the more people remember it.

The more you repeat something, the more people remember it.

The more you repeat something, the more people remember it.

See what I mean?

People talk about songs being catchy when bits of the song end up stuck in their heads. But it turns out half the trick to making something catchy is actually really simple: repeating it a lot. In fact, if you repeat something enough times, people can't help but remember it.

Playing with structure is one way of making this repetition happen – because your chorus or refrain comes back time after time, people stand a much better chance of remembering it. But another way of making repetition happen is repeating things *within* a structure, in a more localized way.

Luckily, these repeated things have a much snappier name — hooks. A hook is a musical or lyrical idea that's repeated enough times to hook you in or hook the song to you — choose whichever visual you like best.

This chapter, though, is just about lyrics. We're going to look at how a lyrical hook — a repeated word or phrase that encapsulates what your song is about — can help make sure what you have to say is clear and easily understood. So let's have at it.

CHOOSING A HOOK

We'll see how you can use a lyrical hook shortly, but first let's talk about what makes a good one.

Here are some great hook examples you probably know:

> Billie Jean
> Happy Birthday
> Walk This Way
> It Wasn't Me

Remember in Chapter 4 when we talked about figuring out what you want your song to be about? Well, the hook you choose is one way you turn this big idea into an actual song.

In general, a good hook is a particular, affirmative expression of what your song is about. A good hook is particular because you want it to encapsulate your song's subject matter pretty explicitly. 'Happy birthday' is a better hook than 'Happy nondescript festivity'. And a good hook is affirmative because you usually don't want to be too cryptic or underhanded in what your hook says. 'Happy birthday' is a better hook than 'It's not your bar mitzvah (It's your birthday)'.

Part of the deal with repetition is that you can repeat anything enough times to be memorable, but if you are going to use your hook liberally throughout your song, it makes sense to choose one that really gets to the heart of what your song is trying to say.

But here's the thing: even if a good hook is a particular, affirmative expression of what your song is about, it's often better to almost hit your song's subject matter on its head than it is to hit it directly. Being too direct can take some of the magic out of what you're saying, and in practice hooks that don't quite say it all normally give you more mileage when you try and incorporate them into a lyric.

Take Shaggy's 'It Wasn't Me'. In this case the hook is the same as the title – we'll talk more about that later – and it just happens to be a great one. By comparison, imagine how much the song would have sucked with a hook like 'I got caught cheating so I denied it' or 'This is a song about infidelity' or just 'I didn't cheat'. 'It wasn't me' is a great hook because it's simple, conversational and something you'd imagine someone saying in that situation.

It's OK that you need the rest of the song's context to understand exactly what 'It Wasn't Me' is about, and that's often part of a hook's charm. But what's most important is that a hook expresses the voice of the person singing your song and isn't just a description of what the song is. That might seem like a subtle distinction but it's the difference between a great song with the hook 'It wasn't me' and a sucky song with the hook 'I didn't cheat'.

Sometimes songwriters go even further and come up with a unique phrase, idea or concept that becomes a song's hook. This is one way you can give a song a unique angle to make it really distinctive, as we've talked about before.

Here are some great examples:

> Total Eclipse of the Heart
> Love Foolosophy
> Single Ladies (Put a Ring on It)
> Out of the Woods

THE ART OF SONGWRITING

As you know by now, interesting new ideas are made up of existing ideas put together in new ways. Like, we know what a heart and an eclipse are, but connecting the two different things is not only a great way of describing feeling lovesick, but it's also a really original way of expressing that idea. And a love foolosophy is a great combination of two words that gives us a clear idea of what kind of love philosophy the song is about.

So if in doubt, try riffing on metaphors or similes that could express your song's situation. What fresh image or idea – and what fresh words that express it – could say it in a way nobody has before? How can you take existing, familiar ideas and create something new and unfamiliar from them?

Plus, don't forget that your hard work in coming up with an original and intriguing hook really pays off, because that's the word or phrase that's going to feature heavily in your song, and it's one of the things people are going to identify your song with most. There are plenty of interesting hooks out there somewhere. All you've got to do is be brave enough to go hunting for them.

You can use pretty much any word or phrase as a hook. If you can find a good way to repeat it as part of a song's lyric, there you go – it can be a hook. But there are a few types of hook worth knowing about if you're not sure where to start. Here are a few of them:

A NAME, PLACE OR THING

> Maria
>
> Miami
>
> Tainted Love

AN EMOTION OR EMOTIONAL STATE

> Happy
>
> Crazy
>
> Sick and Tired

A PHYSICAL STATE OR 'WHEN...' STATEMENT

With You

Waking Up in Vegas

When I Grow Up

A TIME EXPRESSION

Yesterday

Last Summer

Suddenly

A STATEMENT

I'd Die for You

I Luv U Baby

It Wasn't Me

A QUESTION OR INSTRUCTION

Don't You Want Me?

What Can I Do?

Call Me Maybe

A CONVERSATIONAL PHRASE

Excuse Me, Miss

Bitch Please

Hello

USING A HOOK

If half the skill of working with hooks is finding a good one, the other half is about how you use it in your lyric.

INTEGRATING A HOOK SEAMLESSLY

In Chapter 1 we touched on the idea that good craft is supposed to be invisible. Its job is to make a work of art work on a fundamental level, so we can concentrate on what the work of art is trying to say.

Well, with hooks this means integrating them within a lyric in a way that doesn't scream 'HERE'S THE HOOK' every time it comes up. We're trying to write lyrics that look like they just happen to use the hook, not decide on a hook and awkwardly plant loads of other words round it. This is the crafty art of songwriting — making craft a part of the art in a way that doesn't draw attention to itself.

Let's see how this works in The Beatles's 'Yesterday', by John Lennon and Paul McCartney. I've capitalized the hook for emphasis — so it looks a bit like it screams 'HERE'S THE HOOK' every time it appears — but you get the idea.

> YESTERDAY
> All my troubles seem so far away.
> Now it looks as though they're here to stay.
> Oh, I believe in YESTERDAY.
>
> Suddenly
> I'm not half the man I used to be.
> There's a shadow hanging over me.
> Oh, YESTERDAY came suddenly.
>
> Why she had to go,
> I don't know, she wouldn't say.
> I said something wrong,
> Now I long for YESTERDAY.
>
> YESTERDAY
> Love was such an easy game to play.

Now I need a place to hide away.

Oh I believe in YESTERDAY.

One of the reasons 'Yesterday' is such great songwriting is that you could read this lyric aloud without a melody or rhythm and the word 'yesterday' would never seem unnatural, forced or out of place. The word is never shoehorned in just because it's the hook. It sits there naturally within every sentence it's a part of.

Another reason 'Yesterday' works so well is because the hook is featured so many times. It's an AABA form and you'll see the hook is there within each section at least once, and sometimes twice. (It's common not to put the hook in the B of an AABA, but sure, why not?) You'll also notice how the hook comes at the beginning or end of each section where it's much more likely to make an impression.

So the lyric of 'Yesterday' says what it needs to say all while featuring the hook really prominently. This is another of those things that's easy to admire once it's done, but often tough to pull off. It takes practice to do well, and even then it can take plenty of work to come up with natural-sounding lines that incorporate the hook in a significant way. As always, you have to persevere.

FUNDAMENTAL SONGWRITING CHALLENGE #7

Find a hook which gets to the heart of your song's message and incorporate it liberally in your song's lyric.

It's worth adding that 'Yesterday' works because it has just one principal lyrical hook. Sure, there are other words and phrases that are repeated. But the word 'yesterday' is definitely the most important repeated word. You'd have a hard time convincing anyone the hook was something else. This isn't a hard and fast rule – it's not uncommon to find songs that use different hooks in different sections – but it's generally good practice to avoid having two or more hooks fighting each other for attention in any part of your song.

That is, there's a reason *The Lord of the Rings* is about 'one ring to rule them all', not 'lots of different rings to rule over here and over there but maybe not depending how we feel on the day'. See if you can guess it.

WHERE TO PUT A HOOK

Whatever structure you choose, there are plenty of places you can incorporate your hook. In a verse-chorus structure, the hook almost always goes in the chorus, usually right at the beginning or end. In fact, leaving the hook for the chorus – and generally avoiding putting it in the verse – is a common and super effective trick in a verse-chorus structure. In refrain forms, the hook almost always goes in the refrain at the end of each verse. In an AABA form, you have a few more options, but the hook is often in the final line of each A and occasionally at the beginning instead (or, as we saw in 'Yesterday', it sometimes goes in both places).

As usual, there are no rules: there are as many places to put the hook as your imagination can come up with. But if you want a hook to do its job properly, you want to feature it in prominent places and plenty of times throughout your song. Having your chorus or refrain keep coming back helps with this, but as I've said, it's also common to work the hook in a few times within your chorus or refrain.

If you're not sure where to start, I've listed a few common hook patterns you can try on for size below, all featuring the hook more than once. In these patterns, if your hook is a complete phrase, it will probably make up the whole line. Otherwise it'll probably be incorporated within a longer line.

Again, this isn't an exhaustive list, just some of what's possible. See what you think:

Four-line Choruses

1 HOOK	1 HOOK	1 HOOK	1
2	2 HOOK	2	2 HOOK
3 HOOK	3	3	3
4	4	4 HOOK	4 HOOK

Eight-line Choruses

1 HOOK	1 HOOK	1 HOOK	1 HOOK
2	2	2	2
3 HOOK	3	3 HOOK	3 HOOK
4	4	4	4
5	5	5	5
6	6	6	6
7	7	7 HOOK	7
8	8 HOOK	8	8 HOOK

1	1 HOOK	1	1
2	2	2 HOOK	2
3	3 HOOK	3	3
4 HOOK	4	4 HOOK	4
5	5 HOOK	5	5
6	6	6	6
7	7	7	7 HOOK
8 HOOK	8	8 HOOK	8 HOOK

Like I said in the last chapter on structure, eventually you might want to try more adventurous schemes, but these relatively straightforward schemes are worth getting to grips with first.

Also, it's worth noticing how these examples always have some kind of pattern or logic going on. At least one of the hook repetitions is in a conspicuous place at the top or bottom, and there's some kind of repetition or regularity: every other line, every fourth line, or something like that. There's nothing that says you can't put the hook in unpredictable places – like lines 1, 2, 4 and 7 – but since songs are generally built of two- or four-line units, it usually makes sense for there to be some kind of pattern within those divisions.

SO THE HOOK IS THE SAME AS THE TITLE?

Before we bring this chapter to its inevitable and rousing finale, you might have a legitimate question – isn't the hook just the title? Why not use the word 'title' not 'hook'?

Well, no, the title is not always the same as the hook. In fact, we saw this already with 'I Got Rhythm' in Chapter 6.

The lyrical hook is a thing that helps you make your message clear and give your lyric a sense of unity, and the title is a thing people call the song you wrote. In practice, they're often the same but there are various reasons you might not want that to happen.

Sometimes the writer just wants to use a descriptive title – what you might call a 'title-y' title. Well-known examples include Coldplay's 'Hymn for the Weekend', David Bowie's 'Space Oddity', or Michael Jackson's 'Earth Song'.

But – and it's an important but – that doesn't mean none of these songs have a strong lyrical hook, or at least plenty of repetition going on in the lyric. Choosing a different title isn't just a cop-out for not using a hook well. 'Hymn to the Weekend' bases its chorus on the phrase 'Feeling drunk and high'. 'Space Oddity' uses the phrase 'Ground Control to Major Tom' a ton of times. 'Earth Song' kind of uses the words 'ooh' and 'aah' as lyrical hooks that aren't real words – notice how there are no 'ooh's or 'aah's anywhere in the verses to help make that work – and in any case sets those non-words to a clear musical hook. In each case you'll probably agree that the descriptive titles are much more interesting than the words or phrases used as hooks, so that's probably why the writers chose the titles they chose.

In other songs, the published title is just a shortened version of what you could argue is the complete hook. Usually this is about making the title sound snappier or more intriguing, or about avoiding giving away a punchline. Touch and Go's 'Would You...?' sounds way more intriguing (and radio friendly) than 'Would you go to bed with me?'. And Cher's 'Believe' could have been 'Do You Believe in Life After Love?', but you'll probably agree that a punchier one-word title sounds much better.

Whenever you come across songs where the title doesn't match the hook it's worth asking yourself why the writer (or someone else) might have chosen that title instead. Often they're very simple reasons, but they're worth bearing in mind when you're writing your own songs.

So that's the deal with dealing with hooks. Find a word or phrase that gets to the heart of what your song is trying to say, and see how many times you can say it in your song without shoehorning it into places it doesn't really fit. As usual, it's a skill that takes time to master, but with practice it'll become second nature soon enough.

[8]

MUSICAL STYLE

"Words make you think a thought. Music makes you feel a feeling. A song
makes you feel a thought."

E. Y. HARBURG

WHAT IS A SONG ANYWAY?

Here's a good question: why do we write songs? Like, why do we write them in first
place? Why not a poem or a short story or a lively PowerPoint presentation instead?

The answer? Music. What music can do that no other art form can.

That might sound obvious, but it's worth talking about.

Music is the most direct route to the soul. It says nothing in particular, the way
words do, but it is really good at affecting us on a deep and instinctive level. Music
makes us feel things you can't always put into words – and that's kind of its unique
power.

We're an emotional species. We feel things strongly, and by far the best way to
get someone's attention is to affect them emotionally. As Maya Angelou said,

"People will forget what you said, people will forget what you did, but people will never forget how you made them feel."

This is what we get to play with as songwriters. We get to use music to make people feel things. We get to use music to connect with people through their emotions. And if we do it well enough, those people will never forget us, or what we have to say.

And no, this doesn't mean every song has to be a heart-wrenching ballad that leaves everyone an emotional wreck. Other emotions are available. You can use music to make people feel happy, sad, energized, hopeful, chilled out or anything in between. You can make them feel something strongly or you can make them feel it just a bit. The point is that you can make people feel things. And you can use music to do that really well.

That means that when you're trying to decide what your next song is going to be, the most important musical decision you'll make is what you're trying to capture or express through the music of the song. Sure, at some point you'll make decisions on important details like what key to use, whether your tempo should be 80 or 100 beats per minute, whether the strings should play punchy or sustained notes in the bridge. But before any of that, it's your job to decide what kind of emotional or stylistic world you want your song to sit in.

This idea is pretty fundamental. And it's at work in some of your favorite songs, even if you've never noticed it.

Think about those sturdy rocking eighth-note piano chords in Journey's 'Don't Stop Believin''. The ones that say, well, 'don't stop believin''.

Think about those agogo bells rocking back and forth in Britney Spears's '(You Drive Me) Crazy'. The ones that kind of sound like someone going crazy.

Think about the sampled ticking clock in Justin Bieber's 'What Do You Mean?'. Think about how they suit a song that's about wasting time being indecisive, and how they literally turn the line 'Said you're running out of time' into music.

As always, try applying this idea to the songs you love and see what you can learn. I picked some really specific examples to explain how this works but many songs use this idea more generally – in the groove or overall feel, or just in the way a song is trying to be soulful or edgy or dreamy or funky.

But you get the idea: you're trying to get the music of your song to capture your song's big idea in some way. You're trying to make it so that someone who didn't understand the words of your song would still get a sense of what it's about from the music alone.

This is another reason that figuring out all of the stuff we talked about in Chapter 4 is so important. As we've discussed already, in any work of art you want everything to be working together towards some larger goal. So you want what your music is saying to work with what your song is trying to say overall.

It's why the details of what your song is about matter too. There isn't just one style that says 'this is a love song' because there are so many different situations that can make up a love song. An upbeat and straightforward love song doesn't sound the same as a song about the kind of love that drives you insane. A love song sung by a teenager doesn't sound the same as a love song sung by someone in their fifties. Sure, the broad brushstrokes that make up your song's style matter – they matter a lot – but these specifics are important too. People are drawn to the little details that make a song distinctive and individual, so it's worth looking out for opportunities to play with them.

FUNDAMENTAL SONGWRITING CHALLENGE #8

Find a musical style that captures the emotion or mood you want your song to express.

So your job is to use music to support and enhance your song's message – and to use music's emotional power to do that in a really effective way. And this is an art, not a science, of course. Sometimes you have to try out a few different musical styles before you find one that really works. Sometimes what your song is about evolves as you write it, and you decide to alter the music to reflect that. Either way, one thing's really important: a song's style or groove isn't supposed to be just anything. The musical style you choose affects how a song is understood.

And once you've found a song's musical style, a version of that becomes the basic groove for your song. Often you'll end up with different but related grooves for different song sections. Or you'll vary the styles of, say, each verse or chorus slightly for extra interest. In the same way we looked at how structure is about balancing unity and variety, in the best songs the grooves you pick not only exist within the overall world of a song but also grow and develop as the song goes on. Listen out for how this works in the songs you admire.

FINDING YOUR OWN STYLE

We looked at how songs like 'Don't Stop Believin'', '(You Drive Me) Crazy' and 'What Do You Mean?' capture what the songs are about in their music. But here's the thing: they're also completely the sound of Journey, Britney or Justin Bieber. And not just because you can tell who's singing: I'm talking about the style of the song overall.

All of these artists have a style or an identity – even if other people write their songs. And that's what you're trying to do too. It's one of the big ideas of Chapter 3 – if the question is 'What does a love song sound like?', we don't want just any answer, we want *your* answer. We want the love song that you and only you could have written. Great songwriting exists at the intersection of what your song needs from you and what you are uniquely able to give it – and that's your challenge.

So how do you do this? How do you unearth your own musical identity?

Something a bit like this:

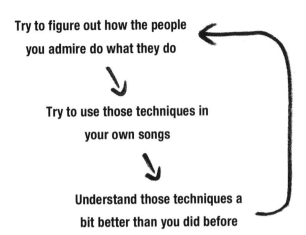

Try to figure out how the people
you admire do what they do

Try to use those techniques in
your own songs

Understand those techniques a
bit better than you did before

This is really just a different version of the cycle we talked about in Chapter 2, but with a twist: this is where you start to inject your personality. Your musical identity is already part of you – and just like we talked about in Chapter 5, you uncover what it sounds like by imitating other songwriters and learning from how they do what they do. And the more you imitate them, the less you end up copying exactly and the more your own personal style comes through. The more you go round the cycle, the more you unearth a bit more of your personal sound.

You're probably some way along this journey already, even if you're just starting out. The trick is just to keep it going and going to let your personal style emerge more and more. And best of all, it's a really fun process: you basically just let your favorite music wash over you, and pick out the bits you like most to use in your own songs. This is often a mostly subconscious process – like with so many things, you just have to relax enough to let it happen.

Of course, this idea applies to lyrics too. In fact, it applies to any kind of art. But it's especially important to making music because there are so many different kinds of music and they all work in similar but distinctive ways. The choices you make about instrumentation are usually different in pop or country or hip-hop. The way you deal with harmony is different in funk or rock or jazz. The drum groove you choose is often a deciding factor in whether your song is a salsa, disco or R&B song.

That means it's up to you to figure out what's common in the genres you want to work in. Read up on things like harmony, instrumentation and composition techniques in those genres. Check out interviews with your favorite artists in magazines, on YouTube and on online music sites. Try to understand how they do what they do – what kind of creative challenges they have to overcome in their particular genre. There are also plenty of places you can get hold of the sheet music for the songs you love, but often you can figure out just as much by listening – really, really listening – to the music you love, to understand better how it works.

> "You can't steal a gift. Charlie Parker gave the world his music, and if you
> can hear it you can have it."
> DIZZY GILLESPIE

As a songwriter it's your job to pack your brain with as much music as you can. Mostly the music you love, but occasionally other music too – it can teach you things the songs you love can't. Listen to as much as you can. Keep an open mind and search out new things. Ask people you admire for new music suggestions.

The more music you know, and the more you build up a conscious and subconscious understanding of what's possible, the more you'll be able to use all that to make exciting and new things.

As usual, you're trying to get inside your favorite artists' brains. You're trying to figure out not just what they do but how and why they do it. As usual, if you want to create like someone else you have to think like them too.

And if you're just starting out, don't worry if what you make sounds kind of derivative. This is not only OK, it's completely normal. Every artist has to start somewhere and it takes years for your own distinctive sound to emerge. This is the same for every artist, I promise: compare an artist's early and late work and you'll hear what I mean. It takes years to unearth your personal style. And, as you know by now, the only way to get there is to keep digging.

[9]

LYRIC ESSENTIALS

If you want to paint landscapes, you get to know what you can do with watercolors. If you want to make pots, you get to know how clay works. If you want to design shoes, you get to know what you can do with leather, rubber and canvas. Whatever you want to create, you get to know how what it's made of works.

As a songwriter, you've got words – and the ideas they express – to play with. And unlike with music, there are some pretty universal principles that make most types of lyrics work well. These principles are what this chapter is about.

MOST OF ALL: FIND THE RIGHT WORDS

As a lyric writer, there are plenty of fancy things you can do with words. You can play with rhyme, repetition, clever wordplay, creative imagery, all sorts of things. And if you want to do all that stuff, that's great. Good for you.

But whatever you do, there's one thing that always matters most: what those words mean. Write that on your forehead or something. It's really important.

The tricks and techniques we're about to discuss are definitely worth knowing about, but they're always secondary. A simple, honest lyric is always more powerful than one that does flashy things but doesn't quite make sense or doesn't quite say what it needs to.

To put it differently – if creativity is discovery, your number one job as a lyricist is to discover the words your song needs to say it best.

FUNDAMENTAL SONGWRITING CHALLENGE #9

Let your lyric say what it needs to say. Use as many lyrical tricks and techniques as you like, but only to support your song's message.

And with words especially, it can take a bit of work to do that discovering. Sometimes you have to say something in a way that isn't quite right before you find a way to say it exactly how you want to. Words work in subtle ways. And often, it's the little details that make all the difference.

You might write something like 'This I can't deny', which is OK but isn't quite how you'd say it in real life. So you might try 'I just can't deny', which is OK too, but is kind of a clichéd expression. So you might end up with 'No, I can't deny' instead, which might happen to fit the world of your song really well.

Or you might write something like 'Let's cheat the game', but pause to realize you don't really cheat a game: you cheat a system or you rig a game (or just play a game). So you'd want to choose whichever of those options can help you say it most clearly and accurately for your particular song.

Or you might write something like 'Check out my car' but realize 'car' is kind of an obvious word. So you might use a thesaurus to come up with 'Check out my automobile', but then put the thesaurus away because it helped you write something that sounded dated even in the 1940s. So you might come up with 'Check out my wheels' instead, because even though the literal meaning of all three options is the same, 'wheels' might be the perfect word in this context.

These are the kinds of decisions you get to make as a lyric writer. These are the kinds of details you get to think about if you want to create a solid, distinctive lyric. As usual, it takes effort and persistence to pull this off, but that's how great lyrics are made.

A LYRIC EXISTS LIVE

If a tree falls in a forest and no one is around to hear it, does it make a sound? Probably. If a lyric sits on a page and nobody sings it, does it make a sound? Probably not.

A lyric really only exists in performance, whether that's a live performance or the recording of a live performance. That might sound obvious, but it's worth saying because words that look great on a page or screen don't necessarily sound great live, and vice versa.

On a page you can use punctuation to clarify what you mean. You can use chapter headings to help point out your structure. You can write long, winding sentences, because if someone doesn't understand them the first time they can go back and read them again. In a lyric you can't do any of these things. Your words have to do all the work to be clear on their own.

When we speak we also do things you don't usually do in writing. We repeat things for emphasis. We add words like 'yeah' or 'um' if they feel natural. We tend to use fewer long or complicated words in speech and we tend to speak less poetically than we write. It's up to you to notice these distinctions and be ready to use them when you write – and you can look at virtually any lyric to see how this works in practice.

KEEP IT CONVERSATIONAL

In fact, a lyric isn't just something that only exists in performance – it's something that's performed by a person. I know, that's obvious too. But it has an important consequence: your job as a lyricist is to capture how people sound when they talk.

There's an art to expressing big and interesting ideas in a way that sounds easy and conversational, and that art is what lyric writing is all about. As Aristotle said, "Think as wise men do, but speak as the common people do." Some people call this 'the poetry of the ordinary' and it's about packing a lyric with meaningful or important ideas in a way that's easy to understand.

Another part of being conversational is trying not to write anything that warps or distorts natural speech. The classic version of this is twisting a line or phrase just to make a rhyme scheme or line structure work. Like this:

> To St Louis he said he'd go,
> But how to get there he didn't know.

Or like this:

> If there's one big problem with the human race:
> We think the grass is always greener in the other place.

The first one sounds kind of poetic but it's not great writing because both lines have their natural word order messed up just to make the rhyme work. People just don't speak like that. The second one sucks even more because it misquotes a common saying to fit a rhyme. It's worth avoiding distortions like these because they make it hard to believe your lyric is being sung by a real person.

Sure, you can play around with an existing phrase to coin a new expression that sounds fresh and inventive – like you might in speech – but if you're just lazily distorting a phrase to fit a structure or rhyme scheme we'll know, I promise. We always know.

Being conversational also means that your lyric doesn't have to read like it's an essay. I've already mentioned how you can use repetitions, slang words or pauses to make a lyric sound like speech. You can even use incomplete sentences to get your point across in a more conversational way:

> Ten pm,
> High heels on.
> Car pulls up,
> She's set 'til dawn.

It's no less clear like this, and as we're about to discuss, leaving out those extra words often also gives your ideas more impact.

KEEP IT SIMPLE

Pablo Picasso said "Art is the elimination of the unnecessary." Just like you wouldn't make a machine with parts that didn't do anything, a work of art works best when everything in it pull its weight, adding something important.

This is especially true in a song lyric. In your average song you have maybe two or three hundred words to get your point across, so you don't want to waste any of them. Unless you need those extra words for some special reason, you don't say 'Is this the way to the place called Amarillo?'. You say 'Is this the way to Amarillo?'. You don't say 'I'm a person who believes deeply in love'. You say 'I'm a believer'.

The trouble is, simplicity is hard to pull off. It's often more complicated than just deleting a few unnecessary words. It's deciding which details to include or leave out. It's saying enough to be clear but not so much that it's too much information.

This is one reason drafting is so important. It let's you take a step back and figure out which ideas are important and which you might not need after all. It's normal for early drafts to come out wordy and overwritten – so one of your jobs in drafting is to cut away anything that doesn't add meaning or isn't an important part of your writing style. Sometimes this is a leap of faith – you often have to cut good things to end up only with great things – but usually what you gain in clarity and focus makes the cutting worth it a hundred times over.

Plus, because a lyric is sung, the music underneath it tends to make what you write richer by default. So you can usually afford to underwrite a lyric more than you might expect. Phrases like 'I don't want to know' or 'Wish you were here' might look boring on the page, but they tend to make great lyrics. Try it and see for yourself.

SPECIFICS MATTER

In a lyric, words matter. But it's the ideas behind those words that matter most. All those different ideas are the building blocks you use to construct a lyric. Words just turn those ideas into something we can understand.

And a lyric tends to be most interesting when those ideas are specific. Just like specific choices for what your song is about matter. Just like specific choices for your song's musical style matter.

In a lyric, this means finding specific images, details and ideas. There are as many ways of doing this as you can imagine, but they turn something bland and generic into something distinctive and really worth paying attention to.

Take this example:

> I love you.
> Yes I do.
> I love you.
> Oh yes, it's true.

Now, it's true that simplicity is important. But there's usually a fine line between simple and generic or boring. So here's one way you could liven up this example:

> I love your six-inch heels,
>
> Your pretty auburn hair.
>
> I love your style, I love your smile,
>
> The sexy way you cock your head and stare.

I stuck with pretty simple images, but can you see the difference it makes? The details start to paint a definite picture. They capture your attention – and spark your imagination – in a way generic ideas don't.

Anyone can chicken out with something bland and generic. Coming up with something particular is more challenging, but specific details make your song stand its ground as something individual and distinctive.

Two common and effective ways of playing with specifics are using similes (when you say something is like something else) and metaphors (when you say something is something else). So you could say 'Baby you're a firework'. Or you could say 'You lived your life like a candle in the wind'. And yes, this conflicts with the idea that lyrics are generally conversational – in real life people don't usually tell you you're a firework – but so long as you avoid things like 'your love is like the resplendent wings of a phoenix', there's some room in a lyric to write in more heightened or poetic speech. In fact, a simple and tasteful metaphor or simile is often a great way to come up with an interesting angle or fresh hook for a song – exactly like in Katy Perry's 'Firework' or Elton John's 'Candle in the Wind'. (As always, keep a look out for your own examples too.)

DON'T ALWAYS HIT THE NAIL ON THE HEAD

Unless you're Tarzan, when you first meet someone you like you don't open with 'Hi, you're hot. Let's date.' You strike up a conversation and express how you feel in more subtle and less direct ways. You pay a compliment, you ask questions or you just flash a cheeky smile. (And if you don't, now's a great time to start.)

In Chapter 7 we looked at how great hooks don't always hit the nail on the head, but this idea applies to lyrics more generally too. Life is more interesting when you say things in more interesting ways. Plus, asking your audience to do a tiny bit of work to understand what you mean makes sure they're involved more deeply than they might be otherwise: asking them to put two and two together makes them engage with what you say much more.

So instead of 'I love you', maybe you say 'I'd cross the ocean for you' or 'I'd give my life for you' or just 'I get so emotional baby, every time I think of you'. Maybe instead of 'you're a dick' you say 'my momma don't like you and she likes everyone'. Maybe instead of 'we've been dating long enough I feel comfortable with you staying over regularly' you say 'you can leave a toothbrush at my place'.

For starters, this is a really great way of giving yourself details to write about. But there's more to it than that: these details help your lyric pack a punch because they're about what people do and not what people say. Actions speak louder than words – in lyrics as well as in real life. And talking about what real-life people do when they think or feel something is a great way of injecting the real world into your songs like we talked about in Chapter 3.

Some people call this 'show don't tell', but that doesn't mean telling is forbidden. (Telling is a kind of showing, after all.) It just means it's always good to look out for opportunities to demonstrate what you mean, and not just spell it out. It just means that showing makes the telling more compelling.

COMING UP WITH MATERIAL: LISTS AND OPPOSITES

Once you've decided what your song is about, your biggest lyrical challenge is coming up with the ideas that flesh that big idea out into an entire song.

There are lots of ways to do this. Sometimes the ideas flow from your song's situation naturally and without much effort. But sometimes the ideas come more slowly, in which case it's worth knowing about two powerful material-generating tricks: creating lists and finding opposites.

Here's a songwriting secret: lots of songs are just lists in disguise. Or just lists not even in disguise. Think of Lou Bega's list of lady friends in 'Mambo No. 5'. Or Alanis Morissette's list of things that aren't really ironic in 'Ironic'. Or the list of things Rick Astley promises not to do in 'Never Gonna Give You Up'.

If a lyric is built of individual ideas, one way to make sure those ideas make sense together is to make them part of a list. Then you can use that list to make up a section of your song, or even a few sections of your song.

If that takes the magic out of lyric writing for you, I apologize, but this is a really neat technique to help you move forward if you get stuck. Just come up with a list of things that are somehow related to your song's central idea. Call it 'Things I love about you' or 'Reasons I'd never leave you' or 'Things I miss about you' if you like. You probably won't give us the list heading as part of the song and you might not even use all of the ideas on the list in the song. And even if you don't end up using the list items directly, that's OK – they might help you put something else together.

Another useful technique is playing with opposites – lists of things that are different or not quite right. In Chapter 6 we looked at ways you can use an opposite or different perspective to create a bridge in a verse-chorus form or a B section in an AABA form. This is exactly the same idea at work on a more local scale.

Usually this means making a point by telling us about the things that aren't right or aren't true before telling us the thing that is. It's a way of clearing space and building anticipation for the big idea. I rewrote my 'What I love about you' example above to demonstrate:

> It's not your eyes, it's not your hair.
> It's not the sexy way you cock your head and stare.
> It's not anything you say or do.
> It's that I get to spend my life with you.

If you want to check out a great real-life example, you'll find the same technique in Cole Porter's 'Who Wants to Be a Millionaire?', which basically lists things the couple singing don't want, before rounding off with ''Cause all I want is you.'

LYRIC STRUCTURE

Creating a solid lyric structure essentially means playing with the order things go in to give them the biggest impact overall. Here are a few tricks you can use to do that.

A STRONG OPENING

Ideally, every idea in your song is a strong one. But it's especially good to open with an especially strong one.

Common techniques to grab your audience's attention from moment one include opening with something dramatic or intriguing, a question, a provocative statement or just a bold image. Here are two examples that do that:

> Did you think I'd never work it out?
> You thought I'd never cotton on?

> She burst into the room –
> Fire in her eyes.

You don't have to start every song with an earth-shattering one-liner, but it's always a good idea to think about how your opening idea draws people in. Keep your ears open to figure out how your favorite writers do this in their songs.

IMPORTANT WORDS OR LINES GO AT THE EDGES

In Chapter 7 we talked about how putting your hook at the beginning or end of your chorus (or both) gives it the most impact. Well, this is also true in general: whether it's the hook or not, it pays to put strong ideas at the edges of sections when you can, and save your less impressive ideas for somewhere inside.

Similarly, the words you put at the end of a line are naturally emphasized more than others – especially if they rhyme. In the same way that comedians get really good at putting the word that makes the joke zing at the end of a line, great lyricists get really good at planting the most important or significant words at the end of lines:

> In any great lyric, let me tell you,
> Weighty words can get lost in the middle, it's true.

Versus:

> Let me tell you as a friend,
> Important words go at the end.

LYRICS THAT PROGRESS OR GROW IN INTENSITY

In a lyric you get to choose what order your ideas come in. So you generally want to choose an order that progresses or grows. Just like in Chapter 8, when we talked about how a musical groove can grow and develop as a song goes on, part of crafting a great lyric structure is starting somewhere solid and taking us somewhere even more exciting as the song goes on.

One of the best ways to do this within or between sections is to put ideas into some kind of ascending order – maybe of length, complexity or emotional weight. Like this:

> She's the kind of girl who'll catch your eye.
> She'll take your hand and make you feel brand new.
> But give her an inch and she'll steal your heart,
> And then there ain't no way out for you.

I'm talking about 'catch your eye', 'take your hand' and 'steal your heart', which work well in this order because what they mean is more emotionally significant each time. There's a definite progression from seeing her for the first time to starting a relationship with her to properly falling for her.

You can even take an existing logical list and make a simple but effective progression out of that. I'm talking about songs like Craig David's 'Seven Days', where the chorus uses the days of the week to hammer home the way a relationship progresses.

A VERSE MASTERPLAN

In a verse-chorus structure, one of your biggest challenges is figuring out what to talk about in the verses. Some people call this the second verse curse – writing a solid first verse but feeling stuck on the second – but, as often, one of the best ways to stop this happening is being one step ahead. This is where a verse masterplan comes in.

Sometimes your verses just talk about different things – they go off on slightly different tangents or pursue slightly different thoughts that are somehow all related to your song's overall message. So if your song idea is 'Life is good when you belong', each verse could focus on different reasons or types of reasons why that's true: it's good to be part of a family, it's good to have friends around, it's good to live in a neighborhood you know well. Or each verse could look forward or back in time: maybe focusing on a time you didn't feel like you belonged, where you belong now or where you'd like to belong in future. Or your second verse could just be a variation of the first: it could take the same structure and shape, even keep a couple of the first verse's phrases intact, and just mix up the ideas or images it brings up.

All kinds of approaches can work – all you're looking for is some kind of organizing principle or theme to give each verse its own identity.

Sometimes, though, there's a more deliberate progression – a sense that each verse really builds on the previous one. There are at least two great ways to do this.

One way is to use the idea of an emotional progression on a bigger scale: to let your second verse go emotionally deeper than the first, or look at something in more detail than the first. So if it's a song about someone missing someone else, maybe your first verse is about general memories but the second goes into more detail about something emotionally more important, like a weekend you spent together.

Another way is to let your verses tell chapters of a larger story, as if your choruses are interludes that separate each chapter. So your first verse could be about two people meeting for the first time, the second about what happened on the second date, and so on. Eminem and Dido's 'Stan' is a great example of this kind of verse masterplan in action.

A TWIST AT THE END

Some songs take the idea of progression even further, waiting until the end of a section or the end of the whole song to throw in a twist or final development – kind of like a Jerry Springer final thought, though less about sleeping with your cousin and more about keeping your song's structure interesting.

This was especially common in old-school AABA forms where writers would tweak a lyric in the final A section to add a kind of conclusion. So – to give you a cheesy example – 'I'm having a great day' might become 'I'm having a great day and it's all because of you' the last time.

This technique works well in verse-chorus structures too. One way of doing this is to save a twist for the end of a chorus:

> She's a dangerous woman.
> She'll get inside your brain.
> She's a dangerous woman.
> She'll steal your heart and drive you insane.
> She'll fill your head with lies and rumors
> And all her crazy stuff.

> Yeah, she's a dangerous woman,
>
> But I just can't get enough.

You'll see how 'But I just can't get enough' flips the whole lyric's meaning. She's not just driving this guy crazy – she's driving this guy crazy and he loves it. It's a more layered idea and much more interesting.

Another kind of twist that you sometimes see in verse-chorus structures is where the final chorus takes on a slightly different meaning from the others. I already mentioned how sometimes later choruses change a line or a word or two, but in this case we're talking about a more substantial change of meaning.

A good example is Bruno Mars's 'When I Was Your Man', which is a regret song about not treating an ex-girlfriend well. The first two choruses open with 'I should've bought you flowers' but the last talks about the new boyfriend and says 'I hope he buys you flowers'. The song goes from looking back to looking forward. It's another simple twist, but you'll see how it gives the end of the song a sense of conclusion.

So there's a handful of ideas and techniques you can use to craft a solid lyric. As usual, they're not a checklist. They're skills and tools you can use when your song calls for them.

In fact, in practice you'll often find these ideas conflicting with each other. I already mentioned how using similes and metaphors can be a great way of coming up with fresh ideas for your song but how they can also make your lyric sound less conversational. And how writing something that's simple but not dull and unspecific can be a bit of a balancing act too.

And you know what? That's exactly how it works. Mastering something as subtle and awesome as lyric writing isn't just having plenty of tools and tricks at your fingertips – it's deciding when and where to use them. It's being confident making a call on which ones to prioritize at any given time. It's knowing sometimes it's OK to sacrifice a bit of a conversational feel to make way for a great metaphor. It's knowing prioritizing simplicity can mean sacrificing detail and prioritizing detail can mean sacrificing simplicity. It's knowing – like we discussed in Chapter 1 – there aren't many perfect choices.

As always, the more you make these kinds of judgments the better you'll get at making them – and the more confident you'll feel about making them. But wherever you're at, if you remember the big idea we started with – to let your lyric say what it needs to say – you can't help but write something that's great.

[10]

RHYME

"I'm just trying to be as honest as possible. If it rhymes so much the better."
LIN-MANUEL MIRANDA

Next up, we're going to keep things technical by talking about rhyme. We'll take a look at some definitions before we see how you can use rhyme in what you create.

It's no secret that rhyme is a really powerful songwriting tool. It helps give a lyric a sense of structure and makes what you write easier to remember. But before we continue, let's be clear that rhyme is not mandatory. You don't have to do it. Plenty of great songs don't rhyme much and some great songs don't rhyme at all.

Like we talked about in Chapter 9, what you say is always most important. You get bonus points if you say something true that also happens to rhyme. But you lose points if you try so hard to rhyme you end up saying things you don't really mean.

FUNDAMENTAL SONGWRITING CHALLENGE #10

Use rhyme to support the meaning and structure of your lyric, and not just for its own sake.

Still, the good news is that once you get skilled enough with rhyme that using it is second nature, it's possible to do both at the same time. You've just got to keep practicing to get there.

SOME DEFINITIONS

Anyone who's listened to at least one song in their life probably has some idea what rhyme is. But as songwriters it's our job to understand how the different types of rhyme work in some detail. So let's take a look.

PERFECT RHYME: MASCULINE, FEMININE AND TRIPLE

Perfect rhyme is the cleanest, purest type of rhyme. Two words are perfect rhymes when two things happen:

One: the final stressed syllable and everything after it is identical in both words.

But, two: the opening consonant sound of that final stressed syllable is different.

If that sounds so technical it left you scratching your head in confusion, don't worry. It'll make more sense with some examples:

> BOAR
>
> CORE
>
> DRAWER
>
> ORE

They're four perfect rhymes. Why? Because one: all of these words have the same -ore sound. But, two: the opening consonant sound is different – whether it's b-, c-, dr- or no sound.

In fact, you'll notice the consonant sound can be a combination of consonant sounds, or no consonants at all. You'll also notice that the spelling of the word isn't important: just how it sounds.

This is pretty straightforward for one-syllable words. But let's go further. Here are some more -ore rhymes:

> GALORE
>
> IGNORE
>
> TROUBADOUR
>
> *ESPRIT DE CORPS*

Rhyme is all about where the stresses or accents lie in the words. Like, you say 'ga-LORE' and 'trou-ba-DOUR', not 'GA-lore' and 'trou-BA-dour'. This is what the 'final stressed syllable' part is about. All these words rhyme because the final stressed syllables match, except for the opening consonant sound of that syllable.

In other words – the number of unstressed syllables at the beginning of a word doesn't affect how it rhymes. You could even rhyme 'BOAR' with 'shoo-ba-de-doo-ba-de-DORE' if you wanted to.

And because the final stressed syllable of these words is the very last syllable, they're called masculine rhymes. Masculine rhymes tend to have a strong and final effect, like a little hammer blow that says 'OK, line's over'. For that reason they're great rhymes to end a section or a song with. They're also great rhymes to choose when you want to keep a lyric simple and not draw too much attention to your rhymes.

When the final stress is on the second-to-last syllable, the words are called feminine rhymes. Like these:

> AWNING
>
> WARNING
>
> GOOD MORNING

In these words the final stress is the penultimate syllable: you say 'AWN-ing' and 'WARN-ing', not 'awn-ING' and 'warn-ING'. And if you try to make one of these words rhyme with a word like 'WING' or 'Bei-JING' it doesn't really work.

Feminine rhymes are a great choice when you want to leave the end of a line open and less final. They have a kind of bounce to them that's perfect for these kinds of lines – especially lines that aren't at the very end of a section.

When the final stress is on the third-to-last syllable, the words are called triple rhymes. Like these:

> TRINITY
>
> AFFINITY
>
> FEMININITY

Again, you can't really rhyme 'TRI-ni-ty' with 'GRIT-ty'. Strictly speaking it's not kosher to rhyme 'TRI-ni-ty' with one-syllable words like 'ME' or 'SEE' either – you don't say 'TRI-ni-TEE' – though lots of writers use rhymes like that and it hasn't brought about the apocalypse just yet.

Triple rhymes aren't used as often as feminine or masculine rhymes, but you'll notice there's a kind of clever and playful effect to them. They're used a lot in genres like rap or comedy songs where wordplay is more important.

And just to clarify: all the rhymes I've mentioned so far are perfect *as well* as being masculine, feminine or triple. Perfect is about how pure the rhymes are. Masculine, feminine and triple is about where the words' stressed syllables are.

NEAR RHYMES

Near rhymes – also called half rhymes or slant rhymes – work exactly the same way as perfect rhymes as far as syllable stresses are concerned, but the sounds that end the words aren't quite the same. Some examples:

DAYS	BRAIN	CITY
HASTE	RAINS	GUILTY

You'll see there's kind of a spectrum: some near rhymes are more perfect that others. In theory, there's no limit to how un-perfect a rhyme can be until it's just 'dog' and 'happy' and they don't rhyme at all.

How pure you want your rhymes to be in any particular song is an aesthetic decision you get to make. In general, the looser the rhymes the more rhyme choices it opens up – making it easier to write rhymed lines that say exactly what you want them to – but if your rhymes are too loose it can make your writing sound sloppy. As always, you get to choose based on what's common in your genre and what you think is best. Some writers swear by perfect rhyme. Some think using only perfect rhymes makes a song sound stuffy and square. Lots of writers keep their options open depending on what they're working on.

COMPOSITE RHYME

Feminine and triple rhymes can be made out of multiple words. These are called composite or mosaic rhymes:

HEY, MAN   COMPANY
NO WAY, MAN   BUMP A KNEE
WHADDAYA SAY, MAN?

Composite rhymes work because it's the sound and the emphases that matter, not the spelling or the number of words. As you'll see with 'company' and 'bump a knee', you can rhyme a single word with multiple words. You could also rhyme 'hey, man' with 'layman' – which you'll tell me isn't quite a perfect rhyme because you say 'LAY-mun' not 'LAY-man' – or a full-on near rhyme like 'raygun'.

But the best thing about composite rhymes is that they're often really easy to come up with and they sound great. All you have to do is take a set of ordinary rhymes and stick a word like 'man' or 'girl' or 'yeah' right after them. So it's not too hard to turn three rhymes like 'woah', 'slow' and 'blow' into something like this:

> Woah, buddy,
>
> Slow, buddy,
>
> Chill before you blow, buddy.

In fact, using composite rhymes like this is a great way of keeping a lyric sounding conversational like we talked about in Chapter 9.

DOUBLE RHYME

Double rhymes happen when two stressed syllables that are independent rhymes sit side by side. That will make more sense with examples:

> You always told me we'd go dancing in the moonlight.
>
> You said we'd make an evening of it soon, right?
>
> C'mon man, are you ready to forfeit?
>
> Watch me blow this game out of its orbit.

When you say words like 'moonlight' and 'soon, right' you can put more-or-less equal stresses on both syllables and create two independent pairs of rhymes – 'MOON-' and 'SOON', '-LIGHT' and 'RIGHT'. Likewise, 'FOR-' rhymes with 'OR-', and '-FEIT' rhymes with '-BIT'. So they're not feminine rhymes (like 'forfeit' and 'morph it'), but they're also much more tightly connected than your average pair of near rhymes.

This only works with words where you can stress both syllables – you can say 'MOON-light' or 'MOON-LIGHT' but you can't really turn 'a-LAS' into 'A-LAS'. And though great double rhymes can take a bit of extra effort to come up with, they can sound really fresh when they're used well. They're common in hip-hop and dance music, though of course you can use them wherever you like.

IDENTITIES

One more definition for the road – identities. They're the perfect rhymes that aren't really. They happen when the final stressed syllable of a word sounds the same but the opening consonant sound is the same too:

DOOR	LEAVE
ADORE	BELIEVE

You'll see what I mean: 'DOOR' and 'a-DORE', 'LEAVE' and 'be-LIEVE'. They don't have anything like the effect of a pair of true rhymes, so lots of songwriters avoid them. This includes homophones – words like 'would' and 'wood' – too.

RHYME SCHEMES

Like with hooks, it's not just about the rhymes you come up with, but where you put them. This is called your rhyme scheme.

Rhymes are most often found at the ends of lines. And just like with hooks, you have a virtually unlimited number of choices for the kinds of rhyme schemes you can create, but let's look a few schemes songs often work with. In my examples, I'm going to use the common notation where matching letters mark lines that rhyme, except for the letter x which marks lines that don't.

SOME COMMON RHYME SCHEMES

We'll start with some four-line units. One of the most common ways to use rhyme is to rhyme every other line, 'hit one miss one' stylee:

It was a Friday night,	(x)
So I took my chance	(a)
When I took your hand	(x)
And said 'let's dance'.	(a)

It's also common to rhyme pairs of neighboring lines, like this:

It was a Friday night,	(a)
And the mood was right.	(a)
So we danced 'til three,	(b)
Just you and me.	(b)

Sometimes you'll also find alternating rhymes, where lines 1 and 3 rhyme, as well as lines 2 and 4. This is harder to pull off and is more common in poetry than song lyrics, but it can be effective in songs too:

It was a Friday night,	(a)
So I took my chance,	(b)
And in the fading light,	(a)
I said 'let's dance'.	(b)

With six lines, it's common to rhyme lines 3 and 6 and leave the others unrhymed, similar to the first four-line example. But if you're feeling adventurous, this is possible too:

It was a Friday night,	(a)
And the mood was right,	(a)
So I decided to take my chance.	(c)
You were standing there	(b)
Just playing with your hair,	(b)
When I came over and said 'let's dance'.	(c)

When this structure is used, often lines 3 and 6 are twice the number of measures as the others – either because those lines are longer (like in this example) or because they're followed by a bit of a gap. This basically makes the whole section eight or sixteen measures long, which, as I hinted at in Chapter 6, is pretty much the norm in songwriting, even for more adventurous sections with unusual line or rhyme patterns. Music seems to gravitate toward sections of multiples of eight – in pretty much all genres – so that's worth bearing in mind.

With eight lines, all kinds of new opportunities open up. Some are just four-line rhymes schemes doubled in size or four-line rhyme schemes twice over. Some are more elaborate.

I'm going to save myself the trouble of writing full examples for all of these, but here are a few eight-line schemes you could play with:

(x)	(x)	(a)	(a)	(a)
(x)	(a)	(a)	(b)	(a)
(x)	(x)	(b)	(a)	(a)
(a)	(a)	(b)	(b)	(c)
(x)	(x)	(c)	(x)	(b)
(x)	(b)	(c)	(c)	(b)
(x)	(x)	(d)	(x)	(b)
(a)	(b)	(d)	(c)	(c)

As usual, this is just a sample of what's possible, not the all-time list of greatest rhyme schemes ever. But like with the hook examples, what's most important to notice is the patterns these rhyme schemes create: either between neighbouring lines, alternating lines or lines that mark the end and the halfway point. Like we saw with hooks, all creating a structure means is creating patterns. So it's worth thinking about the patterns you create if you decide to be more ambitious with your own rhyme schemes and line structures.

INTERNAL RHYMES

As I said already, rhymes are most common at the ends of lines. As well as helping give your rhymes more impact, end rhymes are useful because they help make your line structure clear. They act as a kind of punctuation you can hear. But rhymes appear within lines as well, as what are called internal rhymes.

Here's an example which puts an internal rhyme on line 3 of a four-line section:

It was a Friday night,	(x)
So I took my chance.	(a)
I said 'Hey, girl, (b) whatcha say, girl,	(b)
Come, let's dance.'	(a)

Actually, increasing the pace of your rhymes somewhere in the second half of a section is a really common trick. As you'll hear, internal rhymes kind of bounce along. So giving a lyric a bit of an extra push like that, just before the end, can be a really effective technique.

USING RHYME

With all of the technical stuff covered, let's have a look at how rhyme works in practice.

WRITING RHYMED LINES

Rhyming can be tough. It's challenging to come up with lines that say what they need to say *and* rhyme effortlessly. Because, as you know, making something look effortless often takes a lot of effort.

This is where lots of what we discussed about the creative process in Chapter 5 becomes really important. Writing rhymed lines means discovering lines that make sense and happen to rhyme. In practice, that means discovering lots of lines, words and phrases that say what they need to but don't rhyme – or lots of lines, words and phrases that rhyme but don't say it quite right – first.

One of the best ways to go about this is what some people call free writing or free association. It's pretty much what it says on the tin: you write down as many words, phrases or lines that might work in your song as you can. Don't judge. Don't filter. Just get those words down. Once you come up with some words, phrases or lines that work, see if they spark any other rhyming words, phrases or lines that also work. And rinse and repeat.

Some of what you come up with will be pretty bad. Some of what you come up with will be OK. But some of it will be gold. Your job is to keep going until you have enough key words and phrases that also happen to rhyme that you can start to build a full lyric with them. In fact, often your subconscious brain will start formulating a tidier completed lyric as you get all these rough ideas down.

As I said, the more you do this, the better your brain gets at churning out great rhyming lines. And as you get better, you'll start coming up with full lines and even two-line or four-line chunks more and more easily. You've just got to keep practicing to build up those skills.

FINDING UNUSUAL RHYMES

We talked about this in Chapter 5 too: if you want something to be interesting you have to make it out of interesting things. In a lyric you want to hunt out interesting words and phrases, and you want to use words and ideas that you don't often see together.

So yes, you can spend your entire life using only clichéd and boring rhymes like 'glad' and 'sad', or 'fire' and 'desire', or 'love' and 'turtle dove'. But what kind of a life would that be? Will you look back and say you truly lived?

There are thousands of interesting rhymes that aren't used very often, and they're out there waiting for you. So however you try to come up with a rhymed lyric, it's your job to push yourself away from obvious and overused words and phrases to see if you can throw in a handful of distinctive rhymes in each song.

Here are three specific tricks you can try.

One: using contemporary words or phrases. Like this:

> Don't stay pent up, cold and bitter.
> Let your feelings out on Twitter.

Two: taking advantage of your singer's accent or using colloquial phrases. In Brooklyn this is a perfect rhyme:

> Let me paint a pitcha:
> He's the kind of guy who'll hit ya.

Three: using the names of people, places or things:

> He said he'd never leave her,
> But he ran off to Geneva.

Try 'em out. Don't be shy. Surprise us with what you come up with. And, by the way, there's no harm in using a rhyming dictionary or sites like rhymezone.com to help you find unusual or more interesting rhymes. But don't forget some of the most interesting rhymes – including composite and double rhymes – are the ones you won't find there.

CHOOSING A RHYME SCHEME

We looked at a few different types of rhyme scheme – but how do you go about picking one that works well for your song?

The short answer is it doesn't really matter. No rhyme scheme is automatically better than the others. Sure, they all create slightly different effects, but you can make any of them work, whatever you have to say.

Sometimes a song rhymes alternate or neighboring lines throughout and that's that. But it's also not unusual to find a different rhyme scheme in each of a song's sections – so in a verse-chorus structure, the verse might have one kind of rhyme scheme, and the chorus and the bridge a different one. That's one way of giving each section it's own individual character.

But whatever you choose, you pretty much want to replicate the same rhyme scheme any time a section comes back – which applies especially to your verses, where the lyric is probably new each time. Sure, matching the rhyme scheme between verses makes writing them trickier. But since a section's rhyme scheme is part of its identity, it's nearly always better to keep it consistent throughout your song.

HOW MUCH SHOULD YOU RHYME ANYWAY?

Crocs. Atlantic City. *Speed 2: Cruise Control.* Just because you can do something doesn't necessarily mean you should. So how much should you rhyme?

As usual, you get to make a call. You get to let your song guide you.

Rhyme is a great way to give a lyric a sense of structure and flow. Rhyme makes punchlines funnier and everything easier to remember. But rhyming too much or too often can stop a lyric sounding conversational and natural. Simple, emotional lyrics usually work better without much rhyming. Playful or funny lyrics are often better with plenty of it. It's up to you to find a good balance – but if in doubt too little rhyming is usually better than too much.

[11]

MELODY AND PROSODY

MELODY: SOME FUNDAMENTALS

Whatever kind of music you make, being able to write a solid melody is a great skill to have. But it's especially important when that melody is going to be sung. So let's get some fundamentals down.

VOCAL RANGE

One of the most important melodic things to think about is the vocal range – how high and low your song goes. Most songs sit within what I'm going to call an octave plus a bit – that is, the highest note is something like eight to ten steps above the lowest note. If you're working with a specific performer you can tailor what you write to what they can do, but an octave and a bit is a good maximum range because pretty much every voice can stretch that far. Still, that's not a target: plenty of songs do great things within an octave or less.

How you play with melodic highs and lows for aesthetic reasons is worth considering too. Just like you want your groove to grow and progress as your structure progresses, your vocal melody will have its own journey too. In a verse-chorus structure the chorus often sits in a higher vocal register than the verse – that's one way you can make the chorus a bit more intense than the verse. It's also common for the verse to end in a higher register than where it started: it's the same old trick of beginning somewhere low-ish in intensity and continually outdoing yourself from there. Check out virtually any song ever to see this idea in action.

Some songs make a point of having a single vocal climax – a single highest note somewhere, or a group of highest notes somewhere. In a verse-chorus structure, it's common to find this either toward the end of the bridge or in the vocal riffing in the final chorus (or choruses). You can use this trick within sections too: sometimes a verse or chorus makes a feature out of having the melody peak on a single highest note – often about three quarters of the way through.

MELODIES AND BASSLINES

You probably know about some of music's greatest duos: Frank and Ella, Jay Z and Beyoncé, Sam and Dave. But let's add one more: your melody and your bassline.

No matter what's going on inside your song, your melody and bassline have a special relationship because they're the most important melodic parts, one at (or near) the top, and one at the bottom. And like in any relationship, it's best when the two parts work well together but are also genuinely independent.

First of all, that means you want your bassline and vocal melody to spend plenty of time moving in opposite directions – where one voice goes up as the other goes down. This is called contrary motion and it works like this:

Less Interesting

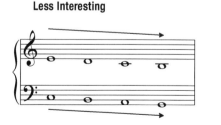

More Interesting

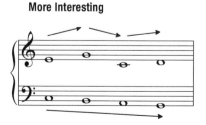

And second of all, it means you generally want your bassline and vocal melody to use different notes as much as possible. Usually your melody moves around more than your bassline does, but if your melody always circles around Cs above C chords and Gs above G chords, you'll make things far more interesting if you mix that up a bit:

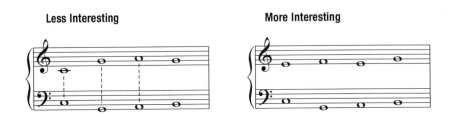

As with everything else, getting good at all of these techniques takes practice – it might take plenty of conscious effort at first, but the more you do it the more it becomes second nature.

MELODIC UNITY

In Chapter 7, on hooks, we looked at how a big part of making something catchy is repetition. This idea applies to writing melodies too, which happens to be all about playing with small melodic ideas called motifs.

Let's take a look.

MELODIC MOTIFS

A melodic motif is a fragment of a melody, made of anything from two or three notes to maybe a dozen. And exactly like a good hook tends to have something distinctive about it, so does a melodic motif – a distinctive shape, a distinctive rhythm, a distinctive melodic leap, or even a combination of the three.

Here are a few examples I just came up with:

The art of great melodic writing is using a small collection of motifs to create a bigger melody. Just like you write a lyric around repetitions of a hook, melodies are built around repetitions of melodic motifs, but with a twist: with music you can develop and vary a motif in ways you can't with words.

To see how this works in practice, let's take a look at the opening bars of Beethoven's Fifth Symphony:

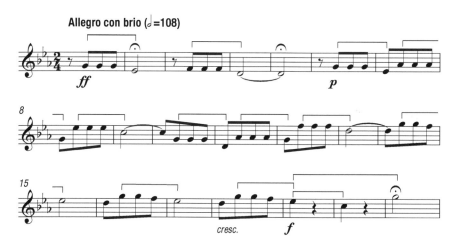

I've given you 21 measures here, and what's so incredible about this extract is that every single note somehow develops from the first 'duh-duh-duh-DUUUUUUH', the principal motif, in measures 1 and 2.

First you get the motif in its pure form. Then you get it again in measures 3 and 4, except it's transposed – shifted in pitch – one step down. Then three different versions of the motif come together to build a complete musical phrase – equivalent to a line or phrase in a lyric – in measures 6 to 9. The first version of the motif is on the same notes as the principal motif, the second on different notes with the melodic shape compressed a bit, and the third on different notes again but the original interval of a third between the two notes stays intact. Measures 10 to 13 respond to this phrase with three more 'duh-duh-duh-duhs' on different notes to fit a new harmony.

From measure 14 onwards, the principal motif is altered by filling the gap – G-G-G-E flat becomes G-G-F-E flat – and an extra D is added to the end. Then, in measures 19 to 21 there are three notes separated by the same distinctive interval of a third that's part of the principal motif.

But don't just take my word for it: dig out a recording. You'll not only see what I mean, you'll hear it too. You'll hear how the whole section is glued together by the opening motif. (Actually, if you keep listening you might hear how the rest of the movement also develops out of this single motif.)

And sure, this kind of motivic unity is extreme. It's rare to find a melody – in a song or a piece of instrumental music – created this religiously from a single motif. (Though the verse of David Bowie's 'Life on Mars' is a great example of a song that does this.)

But you take my point, right? Unified and memorable melodies are about creating a lot of material out of a limited number of building blocks.

In practice, it's much more common to find melodies built from maybe two or three different motifs, and for those motifs to form most but not all of the melodic material.

Let's see how this works in another old-school example, the melody to 'God Save the King'. (Yes, the melody is called 'God Save the King' not 'the Queen'. If you're in the US you can pretend it's called 'My Country 'Tis of Thee' too.)

Here goes:

I took the liberty of marking two important motifs. Let's call one Sonny and one Cher.

Cher, the motif under the solid bracket, is the most straightforward: she's basically three consecutive notes rising or falling, often with that distinctive dotted rhythm. Take a look at the different versions of the motif: sometimes it ascends, sometimes it descends, sometimes the rhythm is slightly altered and sometimes (like in measures 11 and 13) the motif is embellished or buried slightly deeper within the melody. But listen to the melody and you'll hear what's going on: you'll hear the connections between different versions of the core motif.

Sonny, the motif under the dashed bracket, is made up really of just a rhythm: three quarter notes. Sometimes the three notes are the same. Sometimes the last of the three is one step up. You could even argue that measure 5 is a hybrid of both motifs – Cher's melodic shape and Sonny's rhythm – but that's up to you.

There are often a few different ways you could analyze a melody like this, but you get the idea: the entire melody is crafted by playing around with transformations of a few melodic motifs. What's more, this melody is a great example of how a melody can start out in a low-ish register before expanding to include a bigger range of notes: up to D in measure 7 then E in measure 13.

In fact, you might say using both of these ideas – letting a melody develop and expand using a limited number of musical motifs – is good summary of how melodies work in general.

So try applying these two ideas to the songs you love. If you read music, so much the better, but you can also do it just by listening. You're trying to train your brain to get an instinctive sense of how melodies are built and how they grow.

WRITING MELODIES IN PRACTICE

As usual, it's one thing to understand this once someone else has done it – but what about doing it yourself? Do writers really think about all of this stuff when they write melodies? Really?

The honest answer is yes, sort of. Some writers do sit down and work out melodies by playing with motifs like it's a big Sudoku puzzle. They really do. Others rely on their subconscious to create these kinds of connections.

Like with most creative things, it's usually a combination of head and heart. It's about finding a balance between working with motifs consciously but using your instincts to make sure what you're creating has a soul as well as a structure. That usually means you play around with melodic patterns by repeating them, moving them up or down in pitch, mixing up the harmony underneath them and altering or extending them until you end up with a melody that works. You can think in phrases – melodic sentences – too if that helps: write one melodic phrase, then answer it with another, and build from there. Or just focus on a rhythm if that helps instead: don't worry too much about where the melody goes, just use a repeating rhythmic motif or two to keep everything feeling unified.

However you do it, you're aiming to create a web of melodic – or at least rhythmic – connections in what you write. It's those links that glue a melody together and make it memorable and satisfying to listen to. As always, this is something you get better at the more you do it.

If you're primarily a lyricist, these ideas apply to you too. Here's your reward for not skipping this chapter: if you're writing lyrics first, you can help whoever writes the melody big time if you write lines that use similar syllable and accent patterns. Because melodies depend on repetitions like these, if you write lyric lines that all have different syllable and accent patterns, it's going to be much harder to create a great melody that goes with them. Some lyricists who write lyrics first write with a specific rhythm or melody in mind – even if it doesn't end up getting used in the final song. But whatever you do in practice, it's your job as a lyric writer to get a feel for rhythm, accents and syllable counts as much as you would if you had to write the melody yourself.

We've looked at how melodies work when they're sung, but of course these ideas apply to instrumental melodies too. In fact, sometimes instrumental and vocal melodies are related to each other by being based on similar motifs. Sometimes the melodies in different sections of a song are based on similar motifs too – like if the bridge begins with one of the important melodic motifs of the chorus. It's usual to come up with different melodies for each section, of course, but tying them together in subtle ways like that is a neat way of making them feel like they belong within the same song.

So in short, that's how melodies work. Next, let's look at how melodies and words work together.

PROSODY

One of the big ideas of this book is that making a work of art is about making all of the different parts of it work together, to create a stronger effect overall. Prosody – the way words and melody fit together well – is a great example of this.

Because lyrics tend to be most effective when they're conversational, you generally want your melody to sound like a reasonable approximation of speech. That doesn't mean every melodic line has to sound identical to human speech – a song's melody is always going to elevate and twist the words that are attached to it, even just a bit. Sometimes you'll extend words much longer than you would in speech. Sometimes you'll use rhythms that aren't exactly the same as natural speech rhythms. But prosody is about artfully elevating words so we still believe they're coming from a real person – whether in practice the music or the lyric was written first.

In fact, when you commit words to a melody you're making pretty strict choices about how the words are performed and those choices can affect how we understand those words. And that idea is at the heart of how prosody works.

Here are three ways to put that idea into practice.

MATCHING STRESSES

In the last chapter we looked at how rhyme depends on the stresses of words. And rhymed or not, all words have stresses. (At least, in English they do.) If you say something like 'I wandered lonely as a cloud' you'll notice there's a regular stress pattern that goes da-DA da-DA da-DA da-DA.

In song lyrics it's rare to find a regular stress pattern, or meter, like this, but every phrase you come up with will have some kind of a natural stress pattern. And wherever those stresses land, you normally want those stresses to fall on the downbeats in the music – the first beat of each measure, plus the third beat in 4, or the fourth beat in 6.

As the saying goes, you don't want to put the em-PHA-sis on the wrong syl-LAB-le. People don't do it when they speak so you don't want your song to either:

MORE-OR-LESS REALISTIC RHYTHM

When you speak, the words you use also have a kind of intrinsic rhythm. This is to do with the stresses in the words as well as any pauses or emphases you include in what you say. And in the same way you want to avoid writing melodies that make the stresses sound unnatural, you want to avoid choosing a rhythm that radically distorts how you'd say those words in conversation.

For example, with the lyric 'Don't tell me to go', there are all kinds of rhythms you could roll with. You could decide to put 'Don't' or 'go' on longer notes and we wouldn't bat an eyelid because you could imagine someone doing that in speech. You could even extend 'tell' or 'me' too. But you probably wouldn't pick a rhythm that extended the word 'to' because if someone did that in real life it'd sound weird:

Similarly, it's worth making sure you don't end up with any strange or unnatural pauses in the middle of phrases. Since the end of a line typically acts as a kind of punctuation, it would be weird to split a line somewhere you wouldn't split it in speech:

> If there's one thing that
> I like, it's your hat.

It might sound OK it if the first line ran quickly into the second, but if the first line ends with a long note or a gap before the second line, it'd probably sound odd.

This version probably isn't Grammy-winning material, but at least having a bit of a gap between these two lines wouldn't sound unnatural:

> If there's one thing that's great,
> It's your hat, my good mate.

Alternatively, you could try something like this, which gets the same sentiment across and keeps things nice and conversational:

> Well, would you look at that:
> What an awesome hat.

HIGH NOTES EMPHASIZE WEIGHTIER WORDS

As well as emphasizing some syllables more than others, when we talk we also emphasize some words more than others, depending on which words are most important. Try reading that sentence aloud to see which words you stress most.

Generally speaking, higher notes – especially higher notes you get to via a big leap upwards – emphasize the word that's attached to them. For that reason it's worth keeping an eye out for the most important or emotionally charged words in your lyric to see if you can give them a bit of extra emphasis.

At the very least, you want to avoid putting unimportant words like 'at' or 'the' or 'to' on random high notes:

In fact, sometimes changing the words you emphasize can affect what a phrase means. Take the question 'Are you with me?'. If I say 'Are you *with* me?' it's a way of asking if you're on my side. If I say 'Are you with *me*?' it's a way of asking who you're travelling with. So depending which one you mean, you might want to give your melody a little lift to make that clear.

As always, don't just take my word for all of this. Try looking at some of your favorite songs with these ideas in mind to see how prosody works in practice. How is or isn't each song a good example of wedding words and music into a single whole?

There are plenty of examples of great word setting out there, but if you're not sure where to start, three songs worth looking at are Shawn Mendes's 'Treat You Better', Whitney Houston's 'Greatest Love of All', or Adele's 'Hello'.

FUNDAMENTAL SONGWRITING CHALLENGE #11

Use motifs to create a unified and memorable melody. Think about how the melodic choices you make affect how your lyric is understood.

[12]

THE SOUND OF WORDS

In Chapter 9, we looked at crafting a lyric from the point of view of what the words in it mean. But when you perform a lyric, those words have a physical sound too. In this chapter we'll look at how that can affect what you write: how to make your lyric eminently singable as well as how you can play with the way words sound to make your lyric great to listen to.

WRITING SINGABLE LYRICS

If you're lucky to be writing for a really great singer – who might even be yourself – the good news is they'll probably make whatever you write sound great. But part of the skill of songwriting is keeping what you write nice and singable to help your performer do a great job. So let's look at how that's done.

SINGABLE VOWEL SOUNDS

Any syllable – like 'fly', 'eat' or 'ship' – is made up of a central vowel sound, often with one or more consonants at one or both ends. To sing (or speak) these syllables, the voice essentially extends the central vowel sound and slips the necessary consonants in either side. That means if you try and sing a word like 'fly' to a long note, you don't extend the 'fl' sound – because you can't – so you extend the vowel and sing 'flyyyyyyyyyy' to make a longer sound.

This matters in songwriting because some vowel sounds are easier to sing than others. Generally speaking, the open and simple sounds in words like 'car', 'know' and 'true' are easier to extend than the tighter sounds in words like 'cow', 'knee' and 'tray'. (It's no coincidence some of the most popular riffing syllables are 'ah', 'oh' and 'oooh' – they're easy to sing and they sound great.)

Obviously this doesn't override the principle that what your words mean is the most important thing. In the real world you can't write using only the most singable vowels. But with practice, you can train your brain to gravitate to open sounds as much as possible, especially for your melody's long notes. You can also train yourself to spot moments where you could swap words like 'ditch' or 'black' with words like 'leave' or 'dark' to help your lyric sound better when it's performed.

Try saying the lyric phrases 'When I was your man' or 'Somewhere over the rainbow, way up high' and 'I want to break free', and feel for yourself how easy those vowels are to extend. That's what you're trying to train yourself to do in your own lyrics. And if you find yourself writing something like 'If big cats did shots on yachts', it might be better to save that phrase for a haiku or short story instead.

OPEN-ENDED VOWEL SOUNDS

Because extending a syllable to sing it means extending its central vowel sound, words without a final consonant sound are especially well suited for long notes. You can extend a word like 'fly' as long as you want and we don't have to wait to hear the whole word to understand what you're saying. On the other hand, if you tried to extend a word like 'eat' on a really long note it might sound weird because it's not automatically clear whether the word is 'eat' or 'eel' or 'east' until the very last moment.

This applies especially if you want to write a long note at the end of a section or the very end of your song. If you're going to draw out the last note, you want to end with 'I will always love yooooooouuuuu', not 'I will always love Juuuuuuuuude'.

Fortunately, there are plenty of great words with open-ended vowel sounds around. English has words like me, you, I, free, go, be, away – so take your pick.

CONSONANT WATCH

If keeping track of vowels is especially important on your long notes, watching your consonants matters whatever you're writing.

Try saying some different words while you pay attention to what your mouth, teeth and tongue have to do to articulate them, and you'll notice different sounds are made in different ways. Some like 'f', 't' and 'm' are made with the front of the mouth. Some like 'g' and 'h' with the back. Some like 'th' and 'l' particularly involve the tongue. Some like 'b' and 'p' especially involve the lips.

In a nutshell, the more consonants you include in a lyric, and the more neighboring consonants are made using different parts of your mouth, the more effort it takes to sing those words. That means your lyric can turn into a tongue twister if you end up using lots of words and phrases like 'shopping spree', 'nightgown' or 'strewth'. (Sorry, Australia.)

The best way, always, to keep track of this is to practice saying your lyrics out loud. You'll get a sense of where the consonants are backing up and if things are getting tricky you can try to find another way to express the same idea. Obviously this applies all the more if your lyric is going to be sung at some speed.

Before we move on, I'll just say it one last time: what your words mean is much more important than how they sound. There's no competition. It's great when you come up with words that sound great sung, but if it doesn't work out that way, that's

OK too. As you know, writing lyrics means trying to pull off a lot of things, and you can't always pull them off all at once.

But as you also know, the good news is that this all gets easier with practice. Just like you can train your brain to churn out words that both rhyme and say what they need to, the more you become aware of how the way words sound affects your performer, the more you'll find yourself choosing words that use more open vowels and fewer backed-up consonants. I promise. As always, you've just got to stick at it to get better.

WORDS THAT SOUND GREAT TOGETHER

In Chapter 11 we talked about how you can glue an entire melody together by constructing it out of a limited number of melodic motifs. You can't quite do this with words but you can use the way individual words sound to achieve a comparable effect. You might call these sound connections.

Actually, we already looked at rhyme, which is one way this can happen. But there are also other, looser ways words can be connected through the way they sound.

ASSONANCE

Assonance is when the same vowel sound appears several times in quick succession. Like this short song about construction site safety:

> Take a chance on a hat that's harder.

If you say it out loud you'll hear what I mean. The short 'ah' sound in 'a', 'hat', 'that's' and the longer 'ah' in 'chance' and 'har-' work together kind of like a repeated musical motif. So they bind the entire phrase together through the common sound. Plus, you'll hear how all those similar vowels one after another catch your ear in a fun way.

I gave you quite a localized example of assonance here – it's all within one line – but assonance is something you can also play with in a few neighboring lines or even a whole section. And just like rhymes can be perfect or near, you also get an assonant effect with vowel sounds that are similar but not identical.

In fact, if you look again at my example you'll hear that even the vowel sounds that aren't an 'ah' – 'take', 'on' and '-der' – are still pretty close. It all adds up to make the line sound just a bit more enticing.

CONSONANCE

The non-identical twin to assonance, consonance, is the general term for when the same consonant sound appears several times in quick succession. One common type of consonance, where several nearby words begin with the same sound – like 'big bad blowout' – is called alliteration. To demonstrate, here's a hip-hop ode to the Loch Ness Monster:

> He's like a cross-eyed kraken hooked on Krazy Glue.
> Dere ain't a god-damn thing dat dawg won't do.

You'll notice how the first line makes a feature of alliteration of the 'kr' sound, with some bonus 'k' sounds thrown in for good measure. (And just like with rhyme it's only the sound that matters, not the spelling.) In the same way, you'll notice how the second line makes a feature of the 'd' sound.

And just like we saw with assonance, consonance has the strongest effect when the sounds are identical, but similar sounds also work too. You'll see in the second line of my example how the 't', 'g', 'th' and 'w' sounds aren't a world away from the 'd' sound. (Try saying the line and you'll hear it.)

In fact, if you want to get really technical, consonants are often grouped into categories of related sounds like plosives ('b' and 'p'), dentals ('d', 't' and 'n'), fricatives ('f', 'th' and 'v') and sibilants ('s' and 'sh'). It's up to you whether you want to learn their official names, but you get the idea: using similar-sounding consonants near to each other helps make a lyric sound great.

OTHER SOUND CONNECTIONS

Some words have more subtle sound connections between them. Maybe the words sound similar – like 'nature' and 'nurture'. Or maybe they're words that sound identical – like 'know' and 'no' – or words that you can use to mean more than one thing – like 'trip' or 'stand'. Or maybe they're words that contain related syllables or components – like 'tack', 'tackle', 'attack' and 'tax'.

These types of sound connections also have specific technical names – you can look them up if you like – but what's most important is the overall effect: that by using words that are related in sound somehow you can create a kind of aural wordplay:

> Sure, it's not assured on those far-off shores,
> But I can't stand standing here a single moment more.

Again, all those similarities bind the individual words in these lines together, and make them much more fun to listen to.

PARALLEL PHRASING

You can create connections not just between individual words but also between lines by giving them something in common in sound or structure. Here's an example:

> While you've been bleedin' and fightin',
> Well, I've been readin' and writin'.

If you say the two lines out loud you'll hear how they have a lot in common. Not only do the rhymes fall in corresponding places, but 'well' and 'while' also sound similar at the start of the line, plus it's kind of cool how 'you've' and 'I've' are pitted against each other in matching spots. All of these effects make the two lines work really well next to each other.

EXACT REPETITIONS

Words don't have to be different for you to play with the way they sound. It's common in a lot of pop music to repeat a word or part of a word a few times – maybe for emphasis, like in 'My, my, my, Delilah?', or just for fun, like in Rihanna's 'Umbrella, ella, ella, eh, eh eh'. Just like repeating a hook, the repetition helps make what you write more memorable, and it's also a nifty way of using repetition to catch the ear. And maybe best of all, it's a technique that's pretty much unique to songwriting – so ch-ch-ch-ch-check it out in some of your own examples.

It's also common to see this kind of repetition used with a few words, often at the beginning or ends of lines where, as you know by now, it's most noticeable.

When the repetition is at the start of several consecutive lines, the technical term is anaphora, which looks like this:

> I don't want to say goodbye.
> I don't want to see you cry.
> I don't want to go but I know we both can't stay.

Like we talked about in Chapter 9, this song is essentially a list (of things this person doesn't want to do), and that list works even better because each line starts in the same way. The common sound and meaning of those words binds these lines together. You'll also see in this example I threw in a few extra sound connections to bind these words together a bit more: the 'goodbye', 'cry' and 'I' rhymes, the 'say' and 'see' alliteration and the assonance in 'don't', 'go', 'know' and 'both'.

When the repetition is at the end of several consecutive lines, the technical term is epistrophe, which looks like this:

Don't give up.
You can't give up.
I won't let you give up
Until you're sure it's over.

This is a great way of repeating an idea in a way that's more interesting than repeating it exactly. It also gives you the opportunity to make an idea grow in intensity over a few lines – another idea we talked about in Chapter 9 – like this example does.

Sometimes you even find both anaphora and epistrophe happening at the same time, where a line changes slightly in the middle while both ends stay the same:

I'm sorry that I hurt you, babe.
I'm sorry I deserted you, babe.
I'm sorry I let you down, babe,
But I miss you so much right now.

This works like a kind of parallel phrasing, where again the things neighboring lines have in common do a great job of tying those lines together. All that repetition also tends to make what you're saying clearer and easier to understand.

So there's an introduction to some of the aural tricks you can make happen in a lyric. And the good news is that – just like with fresh and unusual rhymes – all kinds of exciting sound connections are out there just waiting to be discovered as you write. Sometimes they'll come to you instinctively. Sometimes you'll write something like 'I can't wait for the weekend' and realize 'I can't wait for the freakin' weekend' says it in a way that sounds much more interesting.

And, as usual, pulling these kinds of sound connections off while you make sure your words say what they need to say is challenging. But it's a skill worth getting to grips with, because these connections elevate what you've written from just any old words to words that are really exciting to listen to.

FUNDAMENTAL SONGWRITING CHALLENGE #12

Use the way words sound to make your lyric easy to sing and exciting to listen to.

[13]

COLLABORATION

Life is one big collaboration. It's about the people you meet, the ideas you share with them and the things you make together.

Whatever kind of songwriter you want to be, working well with other people – and their ideas – is at the heart of being a great writer. And like all skills, it's there to be practiced and mastered.

Collaboration can mean all kinds of things. It can mean co-writing with other songwriters on a particular project. It can mean working with a producer who turns what you've written into a finished track. It can mean working with a performer or event organizer or record label to create something particular for them. It can even mean asking your mom what she thinks of what you've made, or being part of a songwriting workshop, or working with a teacher or mentor. If ideas are thrown back and forth, it's a collaboration.

But whatever kind of collaborative environment you find yourself in, the skills and principles behind doing it well are pretty fundamental.

So let's talk about them.

COLLABORATION FUNDAMENTALS

Collaboration is mostly about communication. It's about how you share ideas with other people and about how you respond to the ideas other people throw at you. We'll look at some specific ways to deal with this soon enough, but first let's get some big-picture principles down.

EVERY COLLABORATION IS DIFFERENT

One of the big ideas of this book is that making something new means doing things differently every time. You don't really know what something is going to be until you do it, and you can make things difficult for yourself if you have too rigid expectations about what the process of making it is supposed to be.

This is especially true when you're working with other people. Different people work in different ways. Different people think in different ways. Different people bring out different parts of you – and you do the same for them in return. Plus, whether you're writing with an old friend, someone you've never written with before, someone who's kind of famous, someone who writes only music or only lyrics or someone who writes both, that's going to make how you work together different. So it pays to be flexible and take each collaboration as it comes.

EVERYONE SHOULD BE WRITING THE SAME SONG

OK, I know. It sounds obvious. But you'd be surprised how easy it is to mess this one up.

Working with other people might be different each time, but however it happens, one of the most crucial decisions you have to make together is what you're supposed to be making in the first place. Four horses can pull a cart four times as well, but if they pull in four different directions they'll pull it apart.

This is another reason that everything I said about song design in Chapter 4 is so important: if deciding what your song is about is a group conversation, it's important that you all have more or less the same picture of what you're trying to create together. Really, it doesn't matter if a song is created by one person or twenty people, only that – like all art – a song works best when it comes from a single, bold vision. As a team, you have to agree on that vision, and finding a way to come up with one overall vision – even if it's not exactly the vision you'd have gone for if you were working solo – is an essential part of collaboration.

BEST IDEA WINS

Your ego doesn't do you any favors as a collaborator. In Chapter 5 we talked about how you have to get your needs out of the way enough to listen to what your song needs. As a collaborator this also means detaching who came up with an idea from the idea itself. Because, really, whose idea it was doesn't matter – only whether it's a good one or not.

That's why, in a collaboration, it's not just your job to have ideas. It's your job to curate them. Just like when you're sketching or drafting something you have to pick out the good ideas and leave the rest, in a collaboration best idea always wins. Whoever came up with it.

IT'S OK TO DISAGREE (ACTUALLY, IT'S GOOD TO)

When a collaboration is working well, two or more people are always going to be smarter together than just one. You all know and think different things, and if you can take the best of everyone's ideas and expertise, you'll end up with something really exciting.

And often, in practice you find that adding more people into the mix creates an exponential effect: you're not just stacking different ideas on top of each other, you're letting more and more ideas interact and combine in ways you'd never have expected. All of those ideas influence each other and ultimately become better and more interesting overall. That's one reason – as we'll talk about – having a respectful and open dialogue is a really important part of collaborating well.

But part of collaboration – part of life – is disagreeing with the people you work with. That's kind of how it goes and kind of part of the process. The skill is learning to use that disagreement to fuel something great. Assuming you're all writing the same song, when two people feel strongly about something they disagree on, they're often both onto something important.

That means it's your job – as a team – to find a solution that works all round. And the good news is that there always is one if you have the time and motivation to look for it. If one of you doesn't want melody A because it's kind of high for your singer but one of you doesn't want melody B because it doesn't set the lyric very well, it doesn't mean it's an either-or that's going to leave someone unhappy. It means you can try melody C, D or E or any other number of solutions until you come up with something that does both. But there's no way to make that happen without having an open conversation and being ready to disagree.

The way you apply these ideas in practice is different depending which side of the exchange you're on, so let's talk separately about what it's like to share and receive ideas.

SHARING IDEAS

CHECK YOUR ATTITUDE

A big part of collaborating well isn't what you say, but how you say it. When you share ideas or give feedback to someone, you're supposed to be supporting them, you're supposed to trust their ability to find their own solutions and you're supposed to say things that help them become a better version of themselves or make their work a better version of itself.

The best feedback is offered 100% unconditionally. That means you're 100% entitled to expect it is heard and understood, but you are 0% entitled to expect it is acted upon. If it's a good idea, it'll stick. If it isn't, it won't. Sure, if you think what you said wasn't understood, by all means try saying it another way. But if you're offering ideas just because you get a buzz from influencing people, you're not doing songwriting right and you're not doing life right.

Plus, collaboration is all about trust. When someone shares a work in progress or half-formulated idea with you, that's kind of an honor. They're making themselves vulnerable by doing that, and it's up to you to respect their courage and openness – whatever you think of what they have to share. The last thing you want is anyone feeling afraid to share what they're thinking or what they've come up with.

BE HONEST

Speaking of trust, part of any successful relationship – in songwriting and in life – is creating an environment where everyone can be honest about what is and isn't working for them. Sometimes that means telling someone something they don't necessarily want to hear. This, my friends, is called real life.

Of course, it's also your responsibility to say what you have to say in the most supportive and forward-looking way you can. But if you become someone who thinks everything is amazing all the time, people will stop taking you seriously pretty quickly. If you're genuinely honest about what isn't working for you, people will listen to you all the more when you talk about what is.

LOOK FORWARD

A big part of being an artist is seeing things that don't quite exist yet, and this applies to giving feedback too. Your most important job in sharing ideas is to take what's already on the table and make it into something better. That means trying to imagine how it could be a better version of what it already is.

Some people say collaborating means never using words like 'no' or 'but', but it's a bit more subtle than that. Like in so many things, it isn't really about the words you use, but the intention behind them: you're trying to say 'OK, where can we take this idea' and not 'That's a bad idea that won't go anywhere'. Your job in giving feedback is to see what kind of amazing places an idea might lead, not shut an idea down before you have chance to see if it has potential. Plenty of great ideas didn't sound that great at some point in their gestation.

One of the best ways to phrase feedback is to ask questions – like 'How about...?', or 'What if you tried...?', or 'Is there a clearer way to...?'. In fact, questions are especially good because giving feedback doesn't necessarily mean having all of the answers right away. Sometimes all you need to do is flag something that's not working and a solution will come soon enough.

EVERY OPINION IS SUBJECTIVE, ESPECIALLY YOURS

OK, your opinion is no more subjective than anyone else's. But since you're the only person who has control of how you express it, here are some things worth thinking about before you do.

The trouble with sharing ideas about art is that virtually everything is an opinion. Of course, when you tell someone what you think about what they've made you're 100% entitled to your opinion. But what you say is likely to go down much better if you acknowledge that it is just one opinion.

Saying something like 'That line sucks' isn't all that helpful because – among other things – it makes it sound like a fact. 'That line didn't work for me', or 'I wonder if there's a better last line' or even 'I think people will be confused by that last line' are much better ways of saying it because they acknowledge that your response is just one response. That way, whoever's on the receiving end of your ideas is less likely to get defensive (or think you're an asshole) and you're not going to get stuck in an endless loop arguing over whether something is categorically great or not. No art is categorically great or terrible or anything like that.

Try it out. Try using phrases like 'I felt...', 'I wasn't sure about...', 'This sounded ... to me' and see what happens. You'll probably get a much more positive reaction than you would otherwise.

Even better – to bring back a big idea from Chapter 1 – if you can phrase your opinion as a cause-and-effect sentence it's even more likely to be helpful. That's the difference between 'The guitar is too loud there' and 'The guitar is so loud there I can't really hear the vocal'. Or 'That line doesn't work' and 'Something about the way that line is phrased is confusing me'. Again, like in this second example, you don't always have to have all the answers, but if you can say what you have to say using a phrase like 'X is creating Y effect for me' your ideas are much more likely to be received well and put to good use. It's about making clear that your response is just one response and giving whoever you're giving feedback to license to use your idea if it's helpful, and not worry about it if it isn't.

Critics and reviewers might write as if there's one objective way of looking at a work of art, but artists – especially artists halfway through making something – are smarter than that. They know that there are as many ways of looking at art as there are people on the planet.

RECEIVING IDEAS

NOT EVERY IDEA WILL BE USEFUL TO YOU

OK. Let's be clear: feedback is a buffet, not a fixed menu.

If you like coleslaw, you take some coleslaw. If you like brie, you take some brie. If you think quiche is an insult to good taste and everything you stand for, you leave it be. You let someone else have it instead.

When you open yourself up to other people's ideas, you'll probably get a pretty impressive buffet. You'll hear some amazing ideas you'd never have thought of on your own. You'll hear some ideas that can help make your song clearer, bolder and more impressive. You'll hear some ideas that sound nice in theory but aren't helpful for the thing you're trying to create. You might even hear some ideas that seem outright crazy and no use to you. (That happens too.)

It's up to you to decide which is which. It's your job to filter those ideas through the big vision of what you're trying to create and figure out how those ideas can help make what you're creating better. That is, the big question isn't 'Is this good or bad advice?', but 'Can I use these ideas to make what I'm creating better?'.

In other words, you don't have to use every idea in the way people suggest you do. You don't have to use every idea, full stop. Getting feedback is just another part of the big idea that creativity is discovery: you're trying to use other people's ideas to help you discover more about what you're creating so you can make it smarter or clearer or bolder.

Sure, this works differently in practice depending who you're hearing from. If the person giving you ideas is your co-writer, your producer or the performer you're writing for, their ideas are going to carry more weight because they have a stake in what you're making. If the person giving you ideas is someone you know well and really respect, their ideas are probably going to have more of an impact on you too. But in general, as a song's creator it's up to you whether and how you act on someone's feedback. If you're the one with skin the game – if it's your job to do the writing and it's your name that goes in the credit – your opinion is supposed to come first. Period.

Of course, sometimes there's a few of you whose job it is to do the writing. In which case, you're supposed to decide how to respond to other people's ideas together. As I said already, it's OK to disagree from time to time, but it's important to agree on the bigger things to get your song working together as a single work of art. And if you do find yourself disagreeing regularly on the big things, you have to decide whether making big compromises on the kind of art you want to make is worth it to maintain that relationship. You might be better off finding other people to work with. We'll talk more about that later.

KEEP YOUR MIND OPEN

At the same time, it's almost always worth hearing people out. Yes, acting on feedback that isn't great for what you're trying to do or acting on feedback you don't understand can do more harm than good. But inspiration can also come from the strangest places.

You know how in the movies the detective spends weeks trying to solve the case, then gets the big breakthrough while making soup or changing a light bulb? Or how the down-and-out guy in some random bar decides to turn his whole life around after overhearing some drunk guy say something crazy? Well, that happens in real life too.

People usually try their best to give good feedback, but not everyone will get what you're trying to do and not everyone will express their ideas in a way that's helpful. Maybe they'll suggest a solution that's not useful to you but in the process help identify what's not working so you can fix it another way. Or maybe with a bit of digging you'll find something useful behind what they're saying – sometimes people are good at spotting what's not working for them but aren't so great at putting it into words.

That's why it's your job to be really good at filtering through other people's ideas to see what you can use. The better you get at that, the more ideas you can take on board, and the better off you'll be for it.

DON'T GET DEFENSIVE

Part of getting feedback on what you've made – part of being an artist in general – is hearing from people who don't like it or just don't get it. And when that happens there's virtually no situation where getting defensive is helpful.

Sure, if someone gives you feedback, you might want to ask them questions to help you understand what they're saying better, or if they just didn't get what you were going for you might try and explain it. This is especially true in collaboration:

sometimes half-formed ideas don't always speak for themselves and that back and forth is part of the process of figuring out whether the idea isn't landing because it's not a great idea or just because you haven't presented it properly yet. But explaining is different from defending.

Because really, getting feedback is just a way of stress testing what you've made. Either it'll help expose the things that aren't working or it'll help convince you that what you did was already strong enough not to need changing. They're both great outcomes.

Not everyone is going to like everything you create, and there isn't much you can do about that. It's not your job to justify or defend every creative decision you make. It's your job to make those decisions, see how people respond and see how that can help you make better decisions in future.

Plus, you are not your work. If someone doesn't like something you made, it doesn't automatically mean they think you're a terrible writer. (At least, it shouldn't.) Great writers write great things, average things and even terrible things. That's part of making art. That's part of taking risks. Don't waste your time getting defensive just because someone disagrees with you. Learn what you can from it and move on.

WORK WITH GREAT PEOPLE

They say you're the average of the five people you hang out with most. In the same way, what you create is going to be the average of the five people whose ideas influence you most. So make good choices.

Work with people you respect. Ask the opinion of people you admire. Seek out people who make things that interest you and think things that inspire you. Surround yourself with great people – everything is easier and better if you do.

And, as you know, this doesn't mean working with people who always agree with you. It's not much fun and there's not much point: if you agree on absolutely everything, for starters you're probably not being honest with each other, and in any case, a big part of collaboration is letting your differences lead you somewhere you couldn't go on your own. Hunt out great people who are different enough from you that your multiple creative minds colliding can only produce something really exciting.

In practice, that doesn't just mean working with people who are skilled at what they do – it means finding people who are a good fit for you. People you share a set of creative values with. People you feel challenged and inspired by when you spend time with them. These are the people who will help you be at your creative best. And whether those people become co-writers, producers, mentors or just people you like to run ideas past, building and investing in quality relationships is one of the most important things you can do as an artist.

And just like dating, you often mess up a collaboration or two before you really get the hang of it. It takes time and your fair share of not getting it right before you get a feel for the kinds of people you're compatible with. So if in doubt, don't be shy. Try working with someone new. See what you can learn from them. Start creating your team and see what remarkable things you can come up with together.

FUNDAMENTAL SONGWRITING CHALLENGE #13

Get good at sharing and receiving ideas, get good at working with other people, and go forth and create something amazing together.

[14]

YOUR VALUES

"Don't you ever let a soul in the world tell you that you can't be exactly who you are."
LADY GAGA

"Every morning when I wake up, I experience an exquisite joy – the joy of being Salvador Dalí – and I ask myself in rapture: what wonderful things is this Salvador Dalí going to accomplish today?"
SALVADOR DALÍ

So far in this book we've focused on the kinds of ideas, principles and tools you can use in pretty much any style of songwriting. But where songwriting – and life in general – gets really interesting is when you start using ideas that don't just apply to everything.

That's right. Welcome to the murky and wonderful realm of beliefs, subjective ideas and matters of personal taste.

Sure, it's part of your job to understand how songs work. But it's also part of your job to use them to do new things. Part of your job as an artist is to think of things that don't exist yet, but should, and then keep working away until they do.

And here's the thing: in a lot of ways this is more important than anything else. That's right: in a lot of ways it's more important to be different at what you do than it is to be good at what you do. Or to put it another way – a big part of doing something well is doing it, well, differently.

That's because, when it comes to creative things, how different and original something is is a big part of what makes it valuable. In other words, if you want to make something that's valuable – and maybe even priceless – you have to be capable of making something nobody else is creating. When the only way someone can get a work of art is from you, that's what makes it valuable – and what makes you, as an artist, valuable too.

Why do people camp out outside the Apple Store for days to be first in line for the latest iPhone? Why were people guessing how *Harry Potter and the Deathly Hallows* would end years before it was even written? How do artists like Taylor Swift or Rammstein or Billy Joel sell out Madison Square Garden in a matter of hours, or even seconds?

Partly because all of these things are good – but also because these things are one of a kind. Nobody but Apple makes anything like the iPhone. There is only one *Harry Potter*. Part of the appeal of seeing your favorite artists perform is that it's a one-of-a-kind experience: it's not quite the same as seeing anyone else.

And sure, not every unique thing becomes a global phenomenon. But it's this kind of uniqueness that bumps an artist up from someone who's just good at what they do to someone who's really worth paying attention to.

And the best news of all is that you're already half way to pulling this off, even if you didn't know it. (Congratulations, by the way.)

You already are unique. Who you are is the sum of everything you've ever experienced, everything you've ever thought and every decision you've ever made. And because nobody else has been through exactly the same things as you, nobody is going to think exactly like you do, nobody is going to have quite the same tastes as you and nobody is going to be exactly like you.

And that means nobody else is capable of creating exactly the same things as you. And nobody else – in the past, present or future – ever will.

The trick is tapping the $&%! into that. That is, the skill isn't finding something you don't have yet, it's harnessing the $&%! out of what you've already got.

So let's talk about that.

BE THE STRONGEST VERSION OF YOURSELF

Remember everything we said about authenticity in Chapters 3 and 4? Well, this is why it's so important. The secret to being interesting is to be new. But the secret to being new is to be, well, you.

If you're already unique, if you're already one of a kind, you just have to show us that. You just have to be yourself, as much as you can and as much as you can get away with.

People respond to authenticity. It doesn't matter if you're writing a song, picking an outfit or giving a wedding speech. If it's a thing that can be done in a creative way, people respond when you do it your way. Authenticity is contagious. The more you do it, the more you remind other people it's OK to do it too. That's true of art as much as it's true of life.

The trouble is, being authentic is hard. It takes practice. And it takes courage. It's much easier to blend in and pretend to be just like everyone else.

Being authentic is hard because it's hard to do it without being criticized. It's hard to do it without someone somewhere telling you you're stupid or you're annoying or you should definitely know better.

"To be nobody-but-yourself – in a world which is doing its best, night and day, to make you everybody else – means to fight the hardest battle which any human being can fight; and never stop fighting."

E. E. CUMMINGS

And that's the thing about making strong choices. Strong choices get on some people's nerves. Strong choices put some people off. Strong choices make some people say 'No, thank you' and occasionally 'No. $&%! you.'

But strong choices are also what make some people say 'Yes, please' and occasionally '$&%! YES, PLEASE'. Strong choices are what make some people go from admirers to superfans. Strong choices are what make some people camp out overnight at the Apple Store, or spend time guessing how your unwritten book is going to end ten years from now, or sit at their computer refreshing eight browser windows to make sure they get tickets to your gig.

That's how it works. You can't be the absolute best thing to one person without being the worst thing to someone else. The things that make you most remarkable and exciting to one person are exactly the same things that make you annoying or embarrassing to someone else.

Beauty is in the eye of the beholder. Ugliness is in the eye of the asshole leaving you a mean YouTube comment at two in the morning. And often – both types of people are totally right. Both types of people are often totally justified in their opinion.

It all depends what's most important to them.

If you agree that things like having solid craft skills, telling great stories and drafting away are what make a song great, you probably got a lot out of this book. If you think things like putting lots of half-naked people in your music video are what make a song great, you probably didn't. (You probably didn't even read this far.)

But that's OK. Your view may well be totally reasonable either way. Right at the start of this book I said it was a lens, a way of looking at songwriting. But it's not *the* lens, *the* way of looking at songwriting. Sure, I used the universal and fundamental ideas that go into making great songs as my starting point, but I'm not going to pretend my way of looking at them is gospel. Not because I don't believe in what I've said – I wouldn't have written it if I didn't – but because there is no gospel. In songwriting or in life.

I've just tried to give you the best version of the songwriting book I wanted to see in the world. And whether you enjoyed it or not says as much about you and what you believe as it does about me and what I believe.

The same is true in what you create. Whatever decisions you make, some people will like them and some people won't. That's why there's no right and wrong when it comes to making creative decisions. That's why you shouldn't act on every single opinion people give you about your art. And that's why there's no such thing as a perfect decision or a perfect work of art.

Some people will admire you and some people will criticize you – while most people completely ignore you – whatever you do. There's no such thing as getting universal approval for every decision you make.

That's why it's better not to look for it.

That's why it's better not to care all that much about what other people think.

I know. That might sound radical and counterintuitive. That might sound contrary to everything your well-meaning parents or teachers or wholesome neighborhood mailman instilled in you as a kid.

But it's true.

Life is about doing things because you think they're good things to do. Not because of the response you think you'll get.

Life is about doing the things you're drawn to do because you're drawn to do them. Not because someone told you to. Not because someone gave you permission. But because you've decided to do them. That's all the permission you need.

And sure, that doesn't mean it's cool not to care *at all* about what other people think. Psychiatrists have words to describe people like that, and they're not very flattering. (You probably have your own words too.) It just means you should care about what you think first. It means you should be aware of how your decisions affect other people, but you shouldn't let that be the most important factor.

Every work of art isn't supposed to be for everyone. It isn't really possible to create a work of art for everyone. Yes, it's possible to create a work of art that millions of people enjoy. It's possible to create a work of art that taps into something popular right now or that resonates with lots of people. But the way to do this isn't to do it because you think it will be popular. It's to do it because it's the kind of art you want to see in the world.

Again, it's your intention that makes all the difference.

Whether it's in the school playground or the Billboard Hot 100 Chart, we can tell when you're trying to do something just to be popular. And we don't like it. It's not a good way to win our respect. Even if we don't agree with every choice you make, in the long run we respect you more for making strong ones. We respect you more for being yourself. We respect you more for having the courage to create the art you want to see in the world.

"Life shrinks or expands in proportion to one's courage."
ANAÏS NIN

And that's why authenticity counts. That's why being bold in what you choose usually matters more than what you choose.

We want you to be the strongest version of the person you are already and not care what we think about it. We want you to have the courage to do that. We want you to encourage and en-courage us to do the same. And the more you do, the more we'll make sure you are rewarded.

YOUR VALUES

All of this, of course, comes down to your values. As it says on the tin, they're the things you value more than anything else. They're the things you believe – and the things you believe in – more than anything else. And they're the things that make you you.

The thing is, you can't have everything. You can't do everything. You can't be really good at everything. There are too many things and you have only so much time and energy and concentration to give to them.

That means you have to prioritize. Just like creativity means turning down OK things so you can say yes to the really great things, life is about rejecting the things you only half want so you can focus on the things you really do want. You have to clear space for the things that matter to you most, and you have to do it actively.

That's because you're always choosing your values, whether you mean to or not. If you get mad at the Starbucks barista who made you a single espresso, not the double you asked for, you're choosing to give your attention to that rather than something else. You're saying that's more important than anything else you could choose to give your attention to at that moment.

And that, by the way, is why being aware of your values is so important. Of course it's annoying not to get the coffee you asked for. You even said please, after all. It's just you only have so much you can pay attention to. It's just your attention is probably better spent on your art, or your family, or your friends, or any number of other, far more important things. It's just that in a few billion years the sun will expand more than a hundred times its current size and destroy all trace of human life on Earth. So maybe the hot drink you ended up with matters less than you thought.

None of this means getting the coffee you wanted isn't at all important. It just means that – with a bit of thought – you'll probably realize there are things that are more important. You'll probably realize there are things that are more worth your time and energy. And that's what having values is all about.

Because here's the thing: if the secret to being the strongest, most decisive, least apologetic version of yourself is finding the courage not to give in to every external pressure, then the better you understand the things you value the easier it'll be to find the courage to stick to them. When you doubt yourself – which you will – it'll help remind you why you're here and what you're trying to do.

So if you haven't already, it's time to start asking yourself these big questions. What's important to you? What are you passionate about? What are you passionate about creating? How can what you make make the world a better – or at least different – place?

> "The closer you come to knowing that you alone create the world of your experience, the more vital it becomes for you to discover just who is doing the creating."
> ERIC MICHA'EL LEVENTHAL

And for the gazillionth time, there are no right and wrong answers. If making rap music is your thing, that's one of your values. If writing love songs is your thing, that's one of your values. If creating new music that fuses heavy metal, Mozart symphonies and Disney showtunes is your thing, that's one of your values too. It's all possible.

Your values don't even have to be styles or genres of music. Your values can be things like a sense of community, or love and compassion, or great relationships. Even having courage and taking risks can be values. It doesn't matter. As long as it's something you believe and believe in, it's one of your values.

As you know, I'm not usually into one-size-fits-all exercises, but here's one I absolutely recommend, precisely because there's never a one-size-fits-all result: figure out your values and turn them into a mission statement.

Call it your manifesto, your credo, your call to arms, if you like, but get it down all the same. Figure out what you really like and find a way of expressing that on a piece of paper, or canvas, or your hallway wall, or wherever you like. Be creative.

Your values will change over time, just like you will change over time, as an artist and a person. But it's a big part of your life's work to know these things. It's a big part of your life's work to know these things so you can do something about them.

Because you should do something about them.

And you should do it sooner rather than later.

You probably know this already, but you're not going to be here forever. Even without the exploding sun doing a number on our planet, none of us is here for very long. We get plenty of opportunities to do our thing, but we don't get unlimited opportunities to do our thing.

You are going to die and there's nothing you can do about it.

Does that scare you? Because it should.

It should scare you into action. It should scare you into living your values without giving a $&%! what other people think. It should scare you into getting the &€#! on with living the life you want to live, and getting the #%£! on with making the things you want to make.

Because sooner or later you won't be able to do that any more.

And that matters.

That matters whether you're Beyoncé at the O2 Arena or Barry at the Rose and Crown's open mic. Your art can change the world, but that doesn't mean you have to change the whole world. It just means changing the bits of the world that are within reach.

You get one life to do that.

Don't waste it.

FUNDAMENTAL SONGWRITING CHALLENGE #14

Don't imitate. Be the strongest, most decisive, least apologetic version of yourself you can be. Let your art make the biggest impact it can.

[15]

PUTTING IT TOGETHER

"Talent is extremely common. What is rare is the willingness to endure the life of the writer."

KURT VONNEGUT

Here's the thing about being an amazing and successful songwriter: pretty much anyone can imagine being one.

Pretty much anyone can picture themselves writing a string of megahits, working with amazing people, making a ton of money — or doing whatever other thing is a fashionable measure of success these days.

But not everyone is prepared to do all the little, tricky and sometimes really tedious things you have to do to make those big, exciting and fun things happen.

Writing is hard, you guys. Being a writer is hard, you guys.

Sure, it's the thrill of making new things. It's the thrill of connecting with other people through what you make. But it's also the uncertainty, it's also the isolation, it's also the staying up until 5am because you have to get something down before you go into the studio first thing tomorrow.

Whenever you try to make something big happen, you're going to be confronted with all kinds of challenges and setbacks you never expected. Life has a funny way of testing you like that – to make sure you really, really want the things you say you do.

And in songwriting, like most things, what makes all the difference is your willingness to put up with the little things you don't necessarily want while you work towards accomplishing the big things you really do.

Here are a few things worth knowing while you make that happen.

BE PROACTIVE

If you want a great life, it's up to you to make it great. It's not up to your parents, your bandmates, your publicist or your fairy godmother. It's up to you.

One of the best things about being a songwriter is that you essentially work for yourself. You decide when and where and how you work. You decide what you want to work on. But that also means you have to motivate yourself to make things happen without relying on someone else to tell you what to do.

You probably remember the chilling words of pop philosopher and Spiderman legal guardian, Uncle Ben: "With great power comes great responsibility." Well, the opposite is true too. If you want more power, more control, more freedom – one way to get it is to take on more responsibility. The more proactive you are about going after what you want, the sooner and better you get it.

So write that song. Join that workshop. Send that demo. Hit up that potential collaborator or performer. You have to start planting seeds now, because some of them are going to take months or even years to grow into something beautiful.

And if you're not sure exactly what to do, that's OK. Nobody is ever completely sure. Just do something. It's almost always better to do the wrong thing and learn something from it than do nothing at all.

BE RESILIENT

Speaking of which, part of the fun of being an artist is that when you do something, you're not always sure how things will turn out. Sometimes you try really hard and get almost nothing back. Sometimes you hardly try at all and everything turns out great. That's just how it works.

Doing something creative and untried means you're probably not going to take the most direct route to get there. Just like making a work of art means messing up and taking plenty of wrong turns, life means messing up and taking wrong turns too. There are always things that go wrong. There are always challenges you never planned on facing. There are always times when you think you're out of your depth or out of your mind or you're just terrified you're trying to pull off the impossible.

And if there are, good. It means you're doing it exactly right. It means you're doing something worthwhile.

Artists learn to be resilient. Artists develop a thick skin. Like we talked about in the last chapter, artists learn to do things – and stick at doing things – because they're worth doing, not because of what they think they'll get from doing them.

The thing is, you can't control how the thing you're working on will be received. You can only focus on making it great in the first place. You can only give your attention to making good choices and seeing what comes of them.

Plus, as an artist, there's not necessarily any relationship between how good you are, how famous you are and how much money you make from your art. There's no High Priestess of Songwriting who makes sure all of the best opportunities go to the most exciting and capable writers. It's a lot more random than that, and there isn't much you can do about it.

That's another reason the more you focus on making great art and the less you worry about what you get back from it, the happier and more creative you'll be. That's not always easy to do, but it is always worth trying.

LIVE LIKE AN ARTIST

Unless you've somehow been reading this book half-asleep, you already know how important this is. Being an artist isn't just about making art. It's about who you are all the goddamn time.

It's up to you to find ways to apply everything you know about being creative to everything you do. Virtually everything can be a creative project if you make it one.

Get good at dressing in your own distinctive way. Or practice telling stories to your friends. Or find daring and unusual things to do on your next vacation. Or talk about your values with the important people in your life. Or throw an interesting new phrase into your next email. Or just practice having courage by doing more things that scare you.

It's no secret that a big part of being a great artist is just practice. So find as many opportunities to do that as you can. They're out there if you keep looking for them.

EMBRACE YOUR INNER INTROVERT

Some artists are the most extroverted and larger-than-life people you'll ever meet. Some, well, aren't. But I don't know a single artist who isn't good at locking themselves away to get some work done when the time comes.

When Gandhi or the Dalai Lama had their greatest revelations were they out at some bar with their mates? Of course not. They went off into the wilderness, they climbed a mountain, they meditated alone. They had to shut out the rest of the world to be alone with their thoughts. And so do you.

Sure, that means being an artist can feel isolating sometimes. But as Lorraine Hansberry said, "The thing that makes you exceptional, if you are at all, is inevitably that which must also make you lonely." Sometimes you have to go adventuring on your own to bring back something remarkable to share with the rest of us.

TAKE ADVANTAGE OF YOUR SELF-DOUBT

Art critic Robert Hughes once said "The greater the artist, the greater the doubt. Perfect confidence is granted to the less talented as a consolation prize."

Part of being a great artist is taking big risks. You know that already. And big risks come with big doubts. You know that already too.

But here's the thing: self-doubt is also really useful. It helps keep you focused. It helps stop you settling for second best. It makes sure you care just enough about what other people think to succeed.

Self-doubt makes you better. So don't fight it. Don't let it get you down. Just let it fuel what you make and keep you at your best.

GET USED TO REJECTION

Lots of people are afraid of rejection – whether they're the one doing the rejecting or the one being rejected – and that doesn't make any sense.

It doesn't make any sense because rejection serves a really important purpose: it keeps things that aren't supposed to go together from going together. Sure, creativity is about putting unexpected things together, but that doesn't mean all things – and all people – are a good fit together. In life, as in anything creative, you have to reject the OK things to make way for great ones. If you want to be at the top of your game, you have to reject any thing, any opportunity and anyone that isn't right for you. There's no other way to do it.

That also means other people ought to reject you when you're not right for them. There's no other way for them to do it. If someone doesn't think you're a good fit for their project, why would you want to work with them? If someone's values aren't compatible with yours, why would you want to write with them? If someone doesn't think your song is right for their band or their competition or their event, why would you want to force it on them? How about showing yourself some self-respect?

It's much better to hold out for opportunities or people who are a really good fit than just settle for anything. No exceptions. You'll have a much better time that way. You'll make much more valuable connections that way. You'll make much better art that way, too.

Like everything else, who is and isn't a good fit really just comes down to compatibility. There's no objectively better or objectively worse. Of course it's going to sting when things don't work out. But that's just your ego, amigo. Don't take it personally. You deserve to find people and opportunities that are a great fit. And you will. You've just got to keep looking.

LET GO OF PERFECTION

Part of being an artist and part of being human is being a work in progress. You are a work in progress. The way you think and write is a work in progress. Everything you create is a work in progress. All of these things could be better. All of these things could be worse. That's just how it is.

Leonardo da Vinci said "Art is never finished, only abandoned." And that's the thing about being creative: yes, you're supposed to keep drafting, revising and polishing something until you can't conceivably make it better. Which sounds simple enough. But in practice, the more you improve or tweak something the more you find to improve or tweak.

You repaint your bedroom but now the living room walls look messy. So you get new wallpaper there but now you see all kinds of scuffs and marks on the hallway floor you'd never noticed before. You can literally go on forever.

Or you can choose a mostly arbitrary point to say 'OK, I'm done'.

There's nothing wrong with striving for perfection. There's nothing wrong with wanting to create perfect things. You just have to remember that actual perfect things don't exist. There might be all of these big ideas about what makes a great song great, but as we've seen, there's no such thing as pulling them all off perfectly, all at once, all the time. You might get close sometimes, but that's definitely not something you can rely on.

One of the things that sucks about being creative is that when you're making something it's easy to focus on all of the things you tried to pull off but didn't quite have time to or couldn't quite figure out how to. It's your job to figure out what's not working and try to fix it, after all. So you're going to be way more aware of these things than anyone else.

But here's the good news: hardly anyone will notice these things. They'll be too busy focusing on what's amazing about what you've made – the things that you totally take for granted because you've been working on something so long those things become second nature to you. They'll probably never know about the things you're not happy with, as long as you don't tell them.

All the things you take for granted about what you make, all the things that are second nature to you, well, they might just be life changing to someone else.

Sometimes it's hard to remember that. But it doesn't mean it's not true.

YOUR NEXT CHALLENGE IS RIGHT IN FRONT OF YOU

If you're always going to be a work in progress, your biggest challenge is to make the most of the work in progress you are right now. That's it. That's all you can do.

Wherever you're at, chances are you're doing amazing things you couldn't do a year ago. Chances are, in a year's time you'll look back at how much you've improved since today. That's how it works.

Sometimes you'll want to take on a challenge that's out of reach. Maybe you want to play more gigs but you don't have enough songs yet. Maybe you want to collaborate on an album but you don't have anyone to write with yet. Maybe you'd love to have a record deal but you only just learnt your fourth chord on the guitar. So don't reach for those things. Figure out what you can reach for and focus on that instead. Take on the challenge that's right in front of you. Do a great job and let it lead to the next, bigger challenge. Then do a great job of that and let it lead to something even bigger.

Your challenge isn't to try and do things that aren't possible just yet. Your challenge isn't to go nuts over what you don't know, what you haven't experienced or what you can't do yet. Your challenge is to keep moving forward. Your challenge is to fill the gaps in what you want to know, experience and be able to do. And your challenge is to use what you *do* know, what you *have* experienced and what you *can* do to make something amazing. However and wherever you can.

AND DON'T FORGET: ART MATTERS

I've said it already: art changes lives. It changes how people think. It changes how people feel. It changes who people are.

The trouble is, lots of people don't believe art is important because the things it does are so hard to measure. How do you measure how many people became better people because they listened to 'Man in the Mirror' or 'If Today Was Your Last Day' or 'Titanium'? How do you measure how many people stuck out their relationship troubles because they heard 'Love Takes Time' or 'If I Can't Have You' or 'The Man Who Can't Be Moved'? Or how do you measure how much better an artist made people's lives – or just their weekends – because they came out to see their show or had their album on in the car or watched them perform on YouTube?

Sure, you can count ticket sales or five-star reviews or video views. But how do you measure all of these little influences and effects a work of art has that make people's lives better?

Exactly. You can't.

And that's what makes art so powerful. That's what makes art matter. And that's exactly why we need people who make it.

Great artists aren't just arts majors who didn't want to get a real job. Great artists might not grow the food you eat or put your arm in a cast when it's broken, but assuming you've got these things covered, great art is one of the things that turn just existing into really living. And since great artists are really good at understanding what living means – like we've been talking about since Chapter 3 – that's why what they make is so important. It teaches us things nothing else can. It helps us feel just that extra bit alive.

And that's why we need you to be an artist. What you create can change lives. But it can't do that if it doesn't exist. It can't do that if you don't find the courage to make it. And it can't do that if you don't believe art matters.

There are plenty of people out there whose lives are ready to be changed by what you create – even if they don't know it yet.

Go find them.

FUNDAMENTAL SONGWRITING CHALLENGE #15

Put this book the $&?%£! down and go make some great songs.
You have everything you need.

WHAT NEXT?

Write something, anything.

Come up with ten new song ideas.

Take one of the big ideas in this book and try it out, even as just an exercise.

Take three of your favorite songs and figure out something new about how they work.

Check out some online or magazine interviews with your favorite artists.

Write your mission statement.

Enjoy the ride.

ABOUT ED

Ed Bell is a songwriter, educator and artist. He's a mix of old-school values and new-school ideas. He was born in Yorkshire in the UK, and educated at Cambridge University and The Royal College of Music in London. He mostly writes music and lyrics for theatre, and lives between Yorkshire, London and the US.

Photo: Laura Luc

Ed has been writing, writing about writing, and teaching writing for over ten years. He created The Song Foundry in 2014. **edbell.com**

THANKS

One of the best things about writing a book is that lots of people help you make it happen but only your name goes on the cover. This is where we set the record straight.

Enormous thanks to Christyn Budzyna, who's been part of this crazy project to create a video series and book since it began nearly three years ago. Thank you for your patience, wisdom and sound advice. Equally huge thanks to the rest of the video series team – Dustin Lee, Robert Freedman, Martin Batchelar, Nick Black and Andrew Simmons – who not only worked tirelessly to make that series happen, but also paved the way for this book in the process. Thanks also to Charlotte Fleming, literary extraordinaire, whose proofing and editing made the book tighter and smarter, and to Kaytie Lee, whose eagle-eyed proofing picked up more last-minute mistakes than I'd like to mention.

Thanks to the friends and family who keep me going on a daily basis. Your encouragement is nice but your faith in me is everything. Thanks in particular to my parents, Jane and Geoff, for their unending support. I wouldn't be here without it.

And thanks most of all to anyone who ever taught me anything, officially or unofficially, directly or indirectly. You are this book. There's at least one of you here on every single page. Finally, special thanks go to Sue Saperia, my first piano teacher, the person who started it all for me, and who left us last summer. If this book inspires even half the number of musicians you did, it will have been worth writing a hundred times over.

You might also know that this book grew out of an online video series called *On Songwriting* we made in 2016. That series was only possible because of the generosity of the people who supported it, and we're endlessly grateful to them. You can find a full list of their names at **thesongfoundry.com/supporters**.

SONG PERMISSIONS

Thanks to the following organizations for giving permission to reprint copyrighted lyrics in this book. You're rockstars.

DELILAH

Words and Music by LES REED and BARRY MASON

Copyright © 1968 Donna Music Ltd. Copyright Renewed. All Rights Administered by Sony/ATV Music Publishing LLC, 424 Church Street, Suite 1200, Nashville, TN 37219. International Copyright Secured. All Rights Reserved. Reprinted by permission of Hal Leonard LLC.

DRIVE BY

Words and Music by PAT MONAHAN, ESPEN LIND and AMUND BJØRKLUND

Copyright © 2012 EMI April Music Inc., Blue Lamp Music and Stellar Songs Ltd. All Rights Administered by Sony/ATV Music Publishing LLC, 424 Church Street, Suite 1200, Nashville, TN 37219. International Copyright Secured. All Rights Reserved. Reprinted by permission of Hal Leonard LLC.

HALLELUJAH

Words and Music by LEONARD COHEN

Copyright © 1985 Sony/ATV Music Publishing LLC. All Rights Administered by Sony/ATV Music Publishing LLC, 424 Church Street, Suite 1200, Nashville, TN 37219. International Copyright Secured. All Rights Reserved. Reprinted by permission of Hal Leonard LLC.

I GOT RHYTHM

Music and Lyrics by GEORGE GERSHWIN and IRA GERSHWIN

Copyright © 1930 (Renewed) WB MUSIC CORP. and IRA GERSHWIN MUSIC. All Rights Administered by WB MUSIC CORP. All Rights Reserved. Used by permission of ALFRED MUSIC.

YESTERDAY

Words and Music by JOHN LENNON and PAUL McCARTNEY

MORE TO READ

Lots of other people's ideas influenced this book. Here's a list of books by some of those people plus some great resources I recommend every songwriter knows about.

For more titles, you can also check out the Song Foundry Bookshelf at **thesongfoundry.com/bookshelf**.

Clement Wood: *The Complete Rhyming Dictionary*, (Dell, 1992)

> A rhyming dictionary is always worth having in reach for those rhyme deadlocks that crop up from time to time. This one comes with *The Poet's Craft Book*, a great old-school introduction to writing techniques.

William Strunk, Jr. & E. B. White: *The Elements of Style*, (Longman, 1999)

> There are at least two reasons this book has been raising the standard of writing the world over for more than fifty years. One: it's really good. Two: it's short enough to read in an afternoon.

Paul Zollo: *Songwriters on Songwriting*, (Da Capo, 2003)

> Paul Zollo's massive book is a collection of conversations with some of songwriting's best. There are all kinds of useful tips, anecdotes and stories and not a Z-list songwriter in sight.

Austin Kleon: *Steal Like an Artist*, (Workman, 2012)

> Austin Kleon's little book will inspire and mess up your creative brain in the most exciting way. A must-read for anyone planning to do anything creative, ever.

Ed Catmull: *Creativity, Inc.*, (Random House, 2014)

> Ed Catmull is the President of Pixar and Disney Animation, two studios that have figured out a thing or two about how creativity and collaboration work. *Creativity, Inc.* talks about some of the life-changing lessons Pixar have learnt over the years.

Seth Godin: *The Purple Cow*, (Portfolio, 2009)

> Seth Godin understands being creative, individual and entrepreneurial probably better than anyone. *The Purple Cow* is his manifesto about taking risks and standing out.

Nassim Nicholas Taleb: *The Black Swan*, (Random House, 2010)

> A Black Swan is an unforeseen event with colossal and far-reaching consequences: exactly the kind artists rely on. Nassim Nicholas Taleb's shrewd observations about chance events and how we deal with them are earth-shattering and life-changing.

Brené Brown: *Daring Greatly*, (Gotham Books, 2012)

> Whatever you decide to do with your life, life is more exciting and more rewarding when you live it courageously. Brené Brown's research into courage and vulnerability is a powerful call to arms for opening up more creativity and self-assurance in everything you do.

Mark Manson: *The Subtle Art of Not Giving a F*ck*, (HarperOne, 2016)

> Life is hard. Things go wrong. And we have to deal with it. Mark Manson's guide to rising above the things that don't matter and tackling the things that do head-on is one of the best personal development books out there. Mark also writes life-changing blog posts at **markmanson.net**.

Made in the USA
Columbia, SC
30 November 2020